Fast Metabolism Diet Cookbook

Over 80 Mouthwatering Recipes Inspired by Haylie
Pomroy's Fast Metabolism Diet Plan

By: Angela Marcum

Table of Contents

Welcome to the Fast Metabolism Diet

If you're on the Fast Metabolism Diet by Haylie Pomroy and you're looking for mouthwatering recipes to incorporate with your diet plan, then you're in luck! This book contains over 80 delicious and healthy recipes for the Fast Metabolism Diet, while following all requirements laid out by Pomroy to ensure proper weight loss.

It's time for you to change your relationship with food. What you eat fuels your body, and when you have the right fuel, your body will function at its optimal performance. You'll lose weight and feel incredible! So, put down that diet shake and toss those chemically-enhanced cookies. This diet is about real, delicious, simple whole foods… and lots of them.

No more starving yourself. No more expensive diet pills or prepackaged meals. By cooking foods that nature intended to go into your body, by making them delicious, and by eating throughout the day, your body will nourish itself back to health.

Rebooting Your Metabolism

It's important to understand the foundation of Haylie Pomroy's Fast Metabolism Diet before you get started, that way you know why you're sticking to it! The basis of the diet is, of course, the process of metabolism.

The metabolic process is what happens when food is transformed either into energy or substance (fat, muscle, blood or bone). You have a metabolism because you're alive! If your metabolism is working right, you'll have the perfect amount of energy available for use, the right amount stored away, and a healthy body.

There are a lot of factors that contribute to an unhealthy metabolism. Have you been feeling overwhelmed with stress? Perhaps you've been on yo-yo diets that deprive you of necessary nutrients, or of food altogether. Our modern society, full of "fake" food products, chemical pollutants, and constant mental pressure along with a commonly sedentary lifestyle can quickly lead to a sluggish metabolism.

When your metabolism is slow, it doesn't know how to properly use the fuel you put into it, so it just gets stored away as fat for later when your body's healthy again. You can see how this starts a vicious cycle.

Well, it's time to break that cycle using food as the medicine to reboot your sluggish metabolism and to fall in love with food again. This diet works on the basis of three phases: On the two days of Phase One, your focus is on fruits and grains. Phase Two is protein and vegetables. Phase Three, you add in healthy fats and nuts. By "shaking up" your eating habits, you essentially confuse your metabolism so that it kicks back in gear.

EAT, MOVE, AND RELAX

Even though there are some fantastic recipes for you in the following pages, here's a little basic reference to help keep you on track for those times when you have to grab something out or throw something together with what you have on hand. This also spells out the exercise or relaxation (yes, relaxation) that goes with each phase.

It's easiest to start your diet plan on a Monday. That way Phase One is Monday and Tuesday, Phase Two is Wednesday and Thursday, and Phase Three is Friday, Saturday, and Sunday!

PHASE ONE

One of these two days is your cardio boost. Take a half hour and push yourself with an aerobic workout, running, swimming, speed-walking, elliptical, or biking. Anything that gets your heart-rape pumping! This burns off stress and a few calories to boot!

Here's the food breakdown for Phase One:

Breakfast- Grain and Fruit

Snack- Fruit

Lunch- Grain, Protein, Fruit, Veggie

Snack- Fruit

Dinner- Grain, Protein, Veggie

PHASE TWO

Time for some strength training. Haylie suggests using heavy weights with fewer reps, rather than light weight with more reps. Your liver will start to build muscle and burn the fat!

Breakfast- Protein and Veggie

Snack- Protein

Lunch- Protein and Veggie

Snack- Protein

Dinner- Protein and Veggie

PHASE THREE

One of the best parts—relaxation! Technically, we're talking about stress-reduction. At least once during this phase, you need to do a stress-reducing activity such as yoga, meditation, message… whatever it takes to get you to a truly relaxed state.

Breakfast- Fruit, Fat/Protein, Grain, Veggie

Snack- Fat/Protein, Veggie (optional)

Lunch- Fat/Protein, Veggie, Fruit

Snack- Fat/Protein, Veggie (optional)

Dinner- Fat/Protein, Veggie, Grain/Starch (optional)

Follow the master list of foods in Haylie Pomroy's Fast Metabolism Diet book, or stick to recipes in this cookbook. The foods in each phase are specifically chosen to address your metabolic slump. Eat five times a day, and don't stray from the plan.

YOUR CHANGING SYSTEM

Any time you change your diet, there will be changes to your entire system. This is what we want, right? Just be sure to listen to your body as you embark on this journey to health.

Some people experience constipation during Phase 2 due to the elimination of grains and fats. It's okay, this is your body reacting and changing… and don't worry, this type of discomfort can be avoided completely:

Try one of these proven effective preventatives:

A cup of Smooth Move tea each night before bed

1,000 mg Vitamin C (corn-free) with a full glass of water at bedtime and in the morning

Psyllium husk powder, as directed on the bottle

If you follow this diet plan, your body and your life will change for the better. Most followers lose close to twenty pounds in 28 days! Congratulations, you're on your way!

*Information to develop recipes was derived from Haylie Pomroy's Fast Metabolism Diet. Before embarking on this or any diet plan, you should always consult your health care professional.

Also note: All recipes serve 1 unless stated otherwise.

PHASE ①...
BREAKFAST!

Green Apple Spinach Breakfast Wrap

PREP TIME: 5 MIN, TOTAL TIME: 10 MIN

Tart green apples combine perfectly with tender baby spinach and green onion in this unusually delicious breakfast burrito perfect for a meal on the run. Tip: Microwave your rice tortilla between two damp sheets of paper towel for easier wrapping.

- ✓ 2 egg whites, beaten
- ✓ 1 rice tortilla
- ✓ ¼ cup baby spinach
- ✓ 1 green onion, thinly sliced
- ✓ 1 small, tart green apple
- ✓ 1 lemon wedge
- ✓ ½ tsp cinnamon
- ✓ Salt and pepper to taste

- Peel, core, and dice the apple. Set a small nonstick omelet pan over medium heat. Toss in the apple, cinnamon, one tablespoon of filtered water and a squeeze of lemon. Cook until apples are tender and fragrant (about one minute).

- Add the egg whites, spinach, and sliced green onion. Cook until eggs are no longer runny, but not browned. Salt and pepper to taste.

- Wrap the filling in a rice tortilla and serve warm.

Spiced Stone Fruit Oatmeal

Spiced Stone Fruit Oatmeal

PREP TIME: 5 MIN + OVERNIGHT, COOK TIME: 10 MIN

The spice combination that recreates the flavor of Jamaican Allspice gives this warm breakfast bowl a spicy undertone that perfectly balances the sweet stone fruits. Hearty and satisfying, you won't miss the maple syrup and brown sugar traditionally served over oatmeal.

- ✓ 1 cup sliced stone fruit (cherries-pits removed, apricots, or peaches)
- ✓ ¼ cup steel-cut oats
- ✓ 1 cup pure filtered water
- ✓ 1 tsp birch xylitol
- ✓ ¼ tsp ground cinnamon
- ✓ ¼ tsp ground nutmeg

- Place the oats in a medium saucepan with one cup of water. Bring to a boil and then remove from heat. Place a lid on the pan and let sit at room temperature overnight.

- In the morning, remove the lid and bring the oats to a boil. Reduce heat and simmer, stirring regularly, until tender (about 7 – 10 minutes).

- While the oats cook, combine stone fruit, spices, xylitol, and one tablespoon filtered water in a small pan set over medium heat. Cook, stirring, until the fruit is softened and fragrant.

- Spoon warm fruit over the oatmeal.

Wild Blueberry Angel Food Cake

PREP TIME: 5 MIN,   TOTAL TIME: 10 MIN

Light and fluffy with a delicately crisp outer layer, this little cake soaks up the berry juices just like real angel food cake. You won't believe you're not eating dessert.

- ✓ 4 egg whites
- ✓ 1 cup frozen wild blueberries
- ✓ ½ cup tapioca starch
- ✓ 2 tbsp brown rice flour
- ✓ 1 packet natural stevia extract
- ✓ Dash nutmeg
- ✓ ½ cup rice milk for serving

- Preheat the oven to 400°F. Whip the egg whites with an electric mixer until they form stiff peaks. Set aside.

- Defrost the blueberries in the microwave (one minute) or a small pot set over low heat (three minutes, stirring). Mix the stevia into the berries. Strain out the juice through a mesh strainer into a small bowl or cup.

- Gently fold the tapioca starch, rice flour, and nutmeg into the egg whites with a rubber spatula. Turn until mixed. Fold in the berries.

- Pour the batter into an oven-proof ceramic ramekin and bake 12 – 14 minutes until the cake is set and spongy. Drizzle with the reserved juice before serving. Enjoy with ½ cup cold rice milk.

Apple Cinnamon Toast

Warm apples and cinnamon make this breakfast taste more like pie than like the healthy start to your day that it actually is! Softer apples, like Macintosh, will cook up softer and quicker than the firmer apple varieties.

- ✓ 1 apple, peeled, cored and diced
- ✓ 1 – 2 tbsp filtered water
- ✓ ½ tsp ground cinnamon
- ✓ ½ tsp birch xylitol
- ✓ 1 slice sprouted grain bread

- In a small saucepan set over medium heat, mix together the peeled and diced apple with the ground cinnamon, birch xylitol, and water. Heat for about five minutes, stirring constantly, until the apples are softened at water is evaporated.

- While the apples cook, toast the bread. Top the toast with the apple cinnamon mixture.

Savory Millet Cakes with Apricot Compote

Savory Millet Cakes with Apricot Compote

PREP TIME: 10 MIN,   TOTAL TIME: 25 MIN

Leftover cooked millet makes this sweet and savory breakfast come together quickly, but taste like you slaved all morning. If you can't find fresh apricots, or if they're not in season, you can use canned but only if they are not canned with sugar. Only apricots canned in their own juices or in pear juice are acceptable.

- ✓ 1 cup cooked millet
- ✓ 3 egg whites
- ✓ 1 green onion, thinly sliced
- ✓ Sea salt and cracked pepper to taste

For the compote:

- ✓ 1 cup fresh apricots, pitted and sliced (about three)
- ✓ 2 tbsp filtered water
- ✓ 1 tbsp tapioca starch
- ✓ 1 tbsp birch xylitol (or to taste)
- ✓ Pinch cinnamon

- For the compote: Place the sliced apricots, tapioca starch, xylitol, water and cinnamon in a medium saucepan. Turn with a wooden spoon to coat.

- Heat over medium heat, stirring regularly, until the apricots are soft and slightly reduced. The sauce should be thickened, about five minutes.

- Remove from heat and set aside.

- For the millet cakes- In a small bowl, thoroughly mix together the cooked millet, egg whites, green onion, sea salt and cracked black pepper.

- Form the batter into three equal balls. Flatten out the balls in the palm of your hand.

- Set a good nonstick pan over medium-high heat. Place the cakes onto the hot pan and cook until browned, about two minutes. Flip and cook the other side. Remove from the pan to a serving plate and top with apricot compote.

Creamy Vanilla Rice Pudding with Fresh Strawberries 20

Creamy Vanilla Rice Pudding with Fresh Strawberries

If you were once a fan of yogurt and fruit for breakfast, you'll love this recipe. The rice milk becomes a creamy, light, delicious substitute for yogurt that will provide your daily grain intake while pairing perfectly with any fresh fruit. Make the pudding the night before so it's chilled and ready to eat in the morning.

- ✓ 1 cup unsweetened rice milk
- ✓ 1 tbsp tapioca starch
- ✓ 1 tbsp birch xylitol
- ✓ 1 tsp pure vanilla extract
- ✓ 1 cup fresh sliced strawberries

- In a small saucepan, whisk together the rice milk, tapioca starch, xylitol and vanilla.
- Turn the burner to low heat. Whisk steadily while the mixture comes to a low boil. It should be just bubbling around the edges.
- Continue whisking until the mixture thickens, about one more minute.
- Pour into a container and cover tightly with plastic wrap to prevent a film from forming on the top. Refrigerate until cold or serve warm with sliced strawberries.

Pineapple Pomegranate Breakfast Smoothie

You need a balanced breakfast to kickstart your metabolism every day, but some days are more rushed in the morning than others. That's when a simple smoothie recipe comes in handy. The unsweetened rice milk provides your grain while the frozen pineapple makes the drink thick, cold, and sweet!

- ✓ 1 cup frozen pineapple chunks
- ✓ 1 cup unsweetened rice milk
- ✓ 2 tbsp pomegranate arills
- ✓ Handful of ice cubes
- ✓ ½ tsp pure vanilla extract
- ✓ Stevia to taste (optional)

- Place all ingredients in your high powered kitchen blender and process until smooth, about three minutes.

- Pour into a tall glass and enjoy.

PHASE (1) ...
LUNCH TIME!

Chicken-Parsnip White Chili

24

Chicken-Parsnip White Chili [serves 4]

Parsnips are a slightly spicy, earthy cousin of the carrot, and they add a nice flavor to this slow-cooked chicken chili. You can spice up the pot a bit by keeping the seeds from the jalapeno in the mix.

- ✓ 1 ½ lbs boneless, skinless chicken breasts
- ✓ 1 15oz can great northern beans
- ✓ 4 cups chicken broth
- ✓ 2 large parsnips, peeled and diced
- ✓ 2 small white yams, peeled and diced
- ✓ 1 red or yellow onion, diced
- ✓ 4 slices turkey bacon
- ✓ ½ cup uncooked quinoa
- ✓ 1 diced fresh jalapeno, or to taste
- ✓ 2 garlic cloves, crushed
- ✓ 1 tbsp cumin
- ✓ 1 tbsp chili powder
- ✓ 1 – 2 tsp sea salt
- ✓ 1 cup fresh chopped cilantro to serve
- ✓ 4 cups (or pieces) Phase 1 fruit

- Set a large pan over medium heat. Cook the turkey bacon for about one minute on each side, until it's starting to crisp. Remove to a cutting board.

- To the same pan, add the chicken breasts and sear on both sides. This is just to release flavors, not to cook the chicken. Remove it to the cutting board.

- With a sharp knife, cut the turkey bacon into small pieces. Place all of the ingredients into a large slow-cooker. Give it a stir, put on the lid, and cook for 6 – 8 hours until the chicken falls apart. If necessary, remove chicken to a cutting board and shred it with a fork, replacing it back into the chili before serving.

- Enjoy this meal with a Phase 1 fruit of choice.

Chickpea and Eggplant Curry [serves 2]

Curry powder is actually a Western invention, but its flavors mimic the Indian spice, garam masala. While the spice variations in curry powder can vary, it's generally a blend of turmeric, cumin, and coriander with some red pepper for spice. This curry dish is just spicy enough, and perfect for the vegan lunch date but filling enough to keep you satisfied until dinner.

- ✓ 2 cups eggplant, peeled and cubed (one large or two small)
- ✓ 2 15oz cans chickpeas (garbanzo beans)
- ✓ 1 cup vegetable broth
- ✓ Large handful mixed baby greens (spinach, kale, chard)
- ✓ 1 cup sweet onion, diced
- ✓ 1/2 cup chopped fresh cilantro
- ✓ 2 tbsp curry powder
- ✓ 1 tbsp lemon juice
- ✓ Sea salt to taste
- ✓ 2 cups cooked brown rice
- ✓ 2 cups sliced mango

- Place the peeled and cubed eggplant, partially drained chickpeas, broth, diced onion, curry powder, lemon juice, sea salt and pepper into a large pan set over medium heat. Bring the broth to a boil, stirring, and then reduce to a simmer for 12 – 16 minutes until eggplant is tender and sauce has thickened.

- Stir in the baby greens and cook for 1 – 2 minutes until greens are wilted.

- Serve over prepared rice (leftovers work great, or get your rice cooking before you start the recipe).

- Garnish with the cilantro and serve with a cup of sliced mango per plate.

Cacao Mango Pulled Pork with Pomegranate Slaw

PREP: 15 MIN, TOTAL TIME: 4 HRS

The surprising flavor of cacao and mango make this pulled pork sandwich far from ordinary. Add the cool, refreshing slaw to the top of your spicy open-faced sandwich or serve it alongside. Either way, the flavors and textures complement each other perfectly.

- ✓ 1 thick-cut boneless pork chop (at least 4 ounces), fat trimmed
- ✓ ¼ cup chicken broth
- ✓ ½ cup diced mango
- ✓ 1 tbsp tomato paste
- ✓ 1 tbsp diced red onion
- ✓ 1 tsp cider vinegar
- ✓ 1 tsp tsp cacao powder
- ✓ ½ tsp each red pepper flakes, birch xylitol, salt, black pepper
- ✓ ½ sprouted grain bagel

For the slaw:

- ✓ 1 cup shredded red cabbage
- ✓ ½ cup shredded jicama
- ✓ ¼ shredded sweet red onion
- ✓ 1 ½ tsp vinegar (white or cider)
- ✓ ½ tangerine, peel, seeds and pith removed
- ✓ 3 tbsp pomegranate arils
- ✓ ½ cup pineapple chunks to serve

- Place the chicken broth, mango, tomato paste, onion, vinegar, cacao powder, and spices into a food processor. Process until smooth, (about one minute). Pour ¼ of the sauce into the bottom of a small slow-cooker. Lay the pork chop over that and pour on the remaining sauce. Cook on high for about four hours or until the pork pulls apart with a fork.

- For the slaw, place the tangerine, vinegar, and a pinch of black pepper into the food processor and set on high until smooth. You can add a little water to this if necessary to thin it out for processing.

- Pour the dressing over the shredded cabbage, onion, and jicama, and mix in the pomegranate arils.

- Serve the pork open-faced on top of the bagel with and the slaw and ½ cup fresh pineapple chunks on the side.

Beef & Asparagus Salad with Roasted Garlic

Beef & Asparagus Salad with Roasted Garlic

PREP: 10 MIN,   TOTAL TIME: 70 MIN

The roasted garlic gives this salad a rich, caramel flavor that pairs well with the bitter crisp asparagus. It takes an hour to bake, but the good news is that you can do it ahead of time and keep it in the refrigerator for up to three days. The soft roasted garlic cloves also make a fantastic spread for your sandwiches!

- ✓ 4 oz roast beef (natural deli slices or sliced from leftover cooked steak)
- ✓ 2 cups packed baby field greens
- ✓ 1 slice sprouted grain bread
- ✓ 5 spears tender asparagus
- ✓ 4 cloves roasted garlic (1 head garlic + 1 tsp chicken broth)
- ✓ 1 tbsp chopped red onion, divided
- ✓ 1 tsp balsamic vinegar
- ✓ Juice of ½ lemon
- ✓ 1 packet pure stevia
- ✓ Sea salt and black pepper to taste
- ✓ 1 cup mixed berries

- To roast the garlic, preheat the oven to 375°F. Remove any loose, papery skin from the outside of a whole garlic head. With a very sharp knife, cut the top off the garlic so that the tips of each clove are exposed. Place the garlic head cut-side-up on a piece of aluminum foil and drizzle the top with one teaspoon of chicken broth. Pull the edges of the foil up and pinch at the top, making a little sack. Bake in the preheated oven for about an hour, until the cloves are soft enough to pop out.

- To make the salad, bring 1 quart of water to a rolling boil. Trim the asparagus and cut into 2-inch pieces. Drop them into the boiling water for about twenty seconds, then quickly remove to a bowl of ice water to cool.

- Toast the bread until very crisp. Sprinkle with salt and cut into one-inch squares.

- Plate the field greens and add the sliced roast beef, par-boiled asparagus, and ½ of the chopped red onion. Carefully remove the roasted garlic from the oven and pop four cloves into the food processor. Add the balsamic vinegar, remaining red onion, lemon juice, and a pinch of black pepper. Process until smooth and pour over the salad. Top with the sprouted grain croutons and serve with a side of mixed berries.

Romaine Salad with Lemon-Hummus Dressing

While true hummus isn't allowed during Phase One because of the tahini (sesame paste) traditionally used to make it, you can get the flavor by combining chickpeas, garlic, and lemon in a simple salad dressing.

- ✓ 2 cups chopped Romaine lettuce

- ✓ 3 radishes, sliced

- ✓ 1 small Roma tomato, diced

- ✓ ½ cup chopped boiled egg whites

- ✓ 1 celery stalk, sliced

- ✓ ¼ cup chopped cucumber

Dressing:

- ✓ ½ cup chickpeas (garbanzo beans), plus a few for garnish

- ✓ Juice from 1 small lemon (about 1/3 cup)

- ✓ ½ tsp birch xylitol

- ✓ 1 clove garlic

- ✓ 1 cup peaches, sliced

- Place the lettuce, radishes, tomato, boiled egg whites, celery, and cucumber into a serving bowl.

- To make the dressing, puree the chickpeas with the lemon juice, xylitol and garlic clove for about thirty seconds until the consistency is smooth with just a few small chunks of chickpea.

- Drizzle the dressing over top of the prepared salad and serve with a cup of sliced peaches, or Phase One fruit of choice.

Granny Smith and Tuna Salad Sandwich

PREP TIME: 10 MIN,   TOTAL TIME: 10 MIN

Not all tuna salad is created equal. The tart Granny Smith apples and fresh lemon-thyme give this sandwich its own unique flair that is fresh and light, while the northern beans replace mayonnaise as a binder to hold everything together.

- ✓ 1 3-oz cans white albacore tuna packed in water
- ✓ ½ Granny Smith apple
- ✓ ¼ cup green onion, sliced
- ✓ 1/4 cup canned great northern beans
- ✓ ½ tsp chopped fresh Lemon Thyme
- ✓ Sea salt and pepper to taste
- ✓ ½ cup sprouts or field greens
- ✓ 1 thick slice tomato
- ✓ ¼ cup shredded carrot
- ✓ ½ sprouted grain bagel
- ✓ 1 cup or piece of Phase One fruit

- Drain the water from the canned tuna. Peel, core, and finely dice the green apple. Trim and slice the onion. Place the tuna in a small bowl and add the great northern beans. Smash them together with a masher or the back of a metal fork until they stick together well. Add the green onion, apple bits, salt, pepper, and chopped lemon thyme and mix.

- Scoop the tuna mixture onto the top of ½ of a toasted sprouted grain bagel and top with sprouts or field greens, shredded carrots and tomato.

- Serve with one cup of Phase One fruit.

Cool Turkey Wrap with Spicy Chipotle Apples

Cool Turkey Wrap with Spicy Chipotle Apples

PREP: 15 MIN, TOTAL TIME: 15 MINUTES

Chipotle chili powder balances the sweetness of the apples and gives your taste buds a nice surprise! If you're making this dish ahead to pack in your lunch, sprinkle the apples with a little bit of fresh lemon juice to keep them from browning.

- ✓ 4 oz natural deli-sliced roasted turkey breast
- ✓ 1 brown rice tortilla
- ✓ ¼ cup peeled and diced cucumbers
- ✓ ¼ cup shredded carrots
- ✓ 1 tsp diced green onion
- ✓ 1 tsp chopped fresh parsley
- ✓ 1 tsp chopped fresh mint leaves
- ✓ ½ cup shredded red leaf lettuce
- ✓ 1 apple, cored, peeled and sliced
- ✓ ½ - 1 tsp chipotle chili powder
- ✓ ½ tsp birch xylitol (if using a tart apple)
- ✓ Squeeze of lemon juice
- ✓ One cup mixed cherry tomatoes and cubed zucchini with a squeeze of lime and fresh cilantro.

- In a small bowl, mix together the cucumbers, carrots, onion, parsley, and mint. Lay the turkey on the tortilla and fill the center with the vegetable mixture. Top with a handful of lettuce and pull the sides up to wrap.

- In another bowl, mix the peeled, sliced apples with chili powder, xylitol and lemon juice (if using). Turn until the apples are evenly coated. Serve cold with the cherry tomato and zucchini salad.

PHASE ①... DINNER IS SERVED!

Shiitake, Leek, and Barley Soup [serves 6]

PREP TIME: 30 MIN, TOTAL TIME: 1 HOUR

This recipe gives traditional mushroom barley soup an Asian twist with Chinese cabbage, shiitake mushrooms and fresh ginger. To add much-needed protein, we also added thin-sliced beef. Slicing raw meat very thin can be tricky, but here's a tip: You can take it to the butcher's counter at your market and ask to have it sliced before purchasing. It makes your prep time and clean-up much easier!

- ✓ 20 oz shiitake mushrooms
- ✓ 1 ½ lb lean beef filet
- ✓ 1 cup dry barley
- ✓ 3 cups water (for cooking barley)
- ✓ 6 cups beef broth (divided)
- ✓ 3 large leeks
- ✓ 2 celery stalks, sliced diagonally
- ✓ 1 cup carrots, cut into matchsticks
- ✓ 3 tbsp tamari
- ✓ 1 tsp grated fresh ginger
- ✓ 3 cups chopped Bok Choy (Chinese cabbage) ribs and leaves, chopped

---

- Bring the barley and 3 cups water to a boil. Cover, reduce heat, and simmer about 30 minutes until the barley is tender and water has been absorbed.

- With a very sharp knife, slice the beef as thin as possible (or have it thin-sliced at the butcher's counter). Clean and trim the leeks and slice them crosswise into very thin rings. Place the beef, mushrooms, leeks, celery, and carrots into a large stock pot or Dutch oven. Sprinkle with 2 - 3 tablespoons of the beef broth and sauté until the beef is cooked and vegetables are tender (about 5 minutes), adding more broth if necessary.

- Add the remaining broth, tamari, Bok Choy and freshly grated ginger. Bring to a simmer over high heat, reduce to low and continue simmering for about 15 minutes. Stir in the barley and serve.

Slow-Cooked Polish Stuffed Cabbage

Slow-Cooked Polish Stuffed Cabbage [serves 4]

PREP TIME: 35 MIN, TOTAL TIME: 10 HRS

Stuffed cabbage, also called Galumpki, is a traditional polish dish that is simple to make but tastes like you slaved over the stove all day.

- ✓ 1 lb lean ground sirloin
- ✓ 1 head green cabbage
- ✓ 1 cup shredded carrots
- ✓ 1 cup diced white onion
- ✓ 2 egg whites
- ✓ ½ cup uncooked brown rice
- ✓ 1 8oz can tomato sauce (puree)

- ✓ ¼ cup apple cider vinegar
- ✓ 2 cloves garlic, crushed
- ✓ 1 tsp salt
- ✓ 2 tsp birch xylitol
- ✓ 1 tsp cracked black pepper (or to taste)
- ✓ 1 lb fresh green beans

- In a large skillet, brown the ground beef with the onion and crushed garlic. Remove from heat and allow to cool for a few minutes before mixing in the dry rice, carrots, and beaten egg whites. Set aside.

- Whisk together the tomato sauce, cider vinegar, birch xylitol, salt and pepper. Set aside. Bring a large pot of water to a rolling boil. Drop the entire head of cabbage into the water. Boil for 5 – 10 minutes until the leaves are tender but not mushy. Drain the water and rinse the cabbage with cold water. Pull off twelve large leaves.

- Remove the cabbage stem and chop up any remaining cabbage and place in the bottom of the slow cooker. Divide the beef mixture evenly between the twelve cabbage leaves. Fold the ends in and roll. Secure with a toothpick if necessary.

- Lay the rolled cabbage into the slow cooker. Stacking them on top of one another is fine. Pour the prepared sauce over the top and cook on low for 8 – 10 hours.

- To cook the green beans, bring a pot of salted water to a boil. Drop in the green beans and boil for about five minutes, or until crisp-tender. Remove with a slotted spoon. Plate three cabbage rolls per person with a scoop of the cabbage chunks over top, and serve with a side of steamed green beans.

Blackened Sole with Spinach-Garlic Quinoa

PREP TIME: 5 MIN,   TOTAL TIME: 35 MIN

Blackened sole sounds like fine dining, but it's actually one of the simplest ways to cook whitefish. All it takes is a pan and some spices. I recommend making a quadruple-batch of this blackened seasoning (1 tsp of each) and saving it in a glass spice jar so you always have it on hand. You can use it to blacken chicken, tuna, and steak as well!

- ✓ 1 sole filet, at least 6 oz (or other whitefish)
- ✓ Blackened Seasoning: ¼ teaspoon each of ground cumin, smoked paprika, dry mustard, black pepper, white pepper, cayenne, paprika, sea salt, dried thyme, dried basil
- ✓ 1/3 cup uncooked quinoa
- ✓ ½ cup chicken broth
- ✓ 2 garlic cloves, minced
- ✓ 1 cup packed fresh baby spinach
- ✓ Sea salt to taste
- ✓ 1 cup mixed field greens with a squeeze of lemon, 1 tsp minced green onion, and cracked black pepper for serving

---

- Bring the quinoa, chicken broth, minced garlic and sea salt to a high simmer. Reduce heat to low, cover, and simmer for about 25 – 30 minutes until all the water is incorporated and the quinoa is fluffy. Remove lid and stir in the baby spinach. Let sit for five minutes.

- Mix together the seasonings in a medium-sized bowl. Heat a nonstick skillet to nearly-smoking over high heat. Drench both sides of the fish filet in the blackened seasoning. Sear 1 – 2 minutes (until blackened) on each side. Serve hot with the spinach-garlic quinoa and the field green salad on the side.

Portabella Buffalo Burger Stack

You can use ground buffalo in place of ground beef in any recipe, giving it a rustic flavor while keeping the same texture and flavor profile as beef. Buffalo is very lean and high in iron and vitamin B12, and since it's typically raised in a more natural environment, it's usually free of any added growth hormones you might find in non-organic beef.

- ✓ 4 oz ground buffalo
- ✓ 2 tbsp finely diced onion
- ✓ 1 tsp tamari
- ✓ 1 egg white, beaten
- ✓ 1 portabella mushroom cap
- ✓ 1 cup packed mixed field greens
- ✓ 1 slice sprouted grain bread
- ✓ For dressing: 1 tbsp tamari, 1 tbsp lemon juice, ½ tsp minced garlic

---

- Whisk together the dressing ingredients and set aside. In a small mixing bowl, blend together the ground buffalo, diced onion, 1 tsp tamari, and the egg white with your clean hands until it's well incorporated. Preheat your grill to medium-high heat.

- Rinse the mushroom cap and remove the stem. Brush with the dressing on both sides. Cook the burger and the mushroom cap next to each other on the grill for about four minutes, flip and cook an additional 3 – 4 minutes. The juices on the burger should run clear, and the mushroom will be darker and somewhat shrunken.

- Toast the bread and set it on the serving plate. Top with the burger, mushroom cap, field greens, and drizzle with remaining dressing. Serve it open-faced, unless you aim to lose more than 40 pounds, in which case you can top with another slice of toast and eat like a burger.

Cajun Sausage & Buckwheat Gumbo   40

Cajun Sausage & Buckwheat Gumbo [serves 2]

PREP TIME: 20 MIN, TOTAL TIME: 40 MIN

Trading out the traditional white rice for buckwheat gives this Cajun dish a hearty, nutty flavor that goes nicely with the spices, peppers, and sausage.

- ✓ 8 oz smoked turkey sausage (nitrate-free)
- ✓ 2 slices turkey bacon, sliced
- ✓ 2 cups diced tomatoes (fresh without skins or canned)
- ✓ 2 cups chicken broth, divided
- ✓ 1/2 cup white onion, diced
- ✓ 1 red bell pepper, diced
- ✓ 1 yellow bell pepper, diced
- ✓ 2 cups zucchini, cut into chunks
- ✓ ¾ cups toasted buckwheat
- ✓ 1 ½ cups filtered water
- ✓ Cajun Seasoning: 1 tsp paprika, ½ tsp garlic powder, ½ tsp dried thyme, ½ tsp onion powder, ½ tsp dried basil, ½ tsp dried oregano, ½ tsp dried mustard, 1 tsp black or white pepper, ½ tsp sea salt, ½ tsp birch xylitol.

- Bring the buckwheat and 1 ½ cups water to a boil. Reduce heat and simmer on low, stirring every few minutes, for 12 – 15 minutes until buckwheat is tender.

- While the buckwheat cooks, cook the turkey bacon in a large skillet over medium heat for about three minutes, stirring regularly. Add the white onion, bell peppers, and turkey sausage and cook until the onion is translucent, about two minutes. Add the chicken broth, tomatoes, Cajun seasoning, and zucchini and bring to a high simmer for about five minutes. Add the cooked buckwheat and simmer another five minutes for flavors to meld.

Garden Veggie Sloppy Sammies [serves 2]

PREP TIME: 15 MIN, TOTAL TIME: 25 MIN

If you like the messy goodness of traditional sloppy Joes, you'll love this veggie-packed low fat version made with turkey burger and lots of chopped peppers, onion, and zucchini. If you're pressed for time, you can substitute the frozen chopped pepper and onion blends found in your grocer's freezer.

- ✓ 8 oz ground turkey burger
- ✓ ½ onion, diced
- ✓ 2 cloves garlic, crushed
- ✓ 1 red bell pepper, diced
- ✓ 1 green bell pepper, diced
- ✓ 1 small zucchini, diced
- ✓ 1/2 cup natural tomato puree, no sugar added
- ✓ 3 tbsp natural tomato paste, no sugar added
- ✓ 1 tsp birch xylitol
- ✓ ½ tsp each: chili powder, onion powder, cumin, nutmeg, sea salt, black pepper
- ✓ 1 sprouted grain bagel, split

- Place the ground turkey, peppers, onion, garlic, and zucchini into a large nonstick skillet set over medium heat. Cook, stirring constantly, until vegetables are soft and turkey is cooked through (about eight minutes). Add tomato puree, tomato paste, xylitol and spices. Turn down heat and simmer five to ten minutes to let the flavors blend.

- Serve on top of sprouted grain bagel.

Summer Chicken Spring Rolls [serves 2]

PREP TIME: 15 MIN, TOTAL TIME: 15 MIN

You can get all the lovely flavors of Asian spring rolls without all the fat by simply not frying them! The brown rice wrappers are light and delicate, letting the crunchy, savory foods shine for themselves. Brown rice wrappers can be found at health food stores and online.

- ✓ 4 brown rice wrappers
- ✓ 8 ounces cooked chicken breast
- ✓ 2 green onions, thinly sliced
- ✓ 2 cups packaged cabbage slaw (with carrots)
- ✓ 1 tsp freshly grated ginger
- ✓ 1 clove garlic, crushed

- ✓ Juice from half of a lemon
- ✓ 2 tbsp tamari
- ✓ 1 tbsp rice vinegar
- ✓ 1 drop liquid stevia
- ✓ Pinch freshly grated garlic
- ✓ 2 cups field greens, for serving

- Finely dice the chicken breast and place in a large mixing bowl.

- Add the cabbage slaw, green onions, grated ginger, lemon juice, and garlic. Mix well with a wooden spoon, mashing down the mixture slightly with the back of the spoon so everything starts to stick slightly.

- To make the dipping sauce, whisk together the tamari, rice vinegar, stevia and pinch of garlic in a small bowl. Set aside.

- Fill a pie pan half way with lukewarm water. Lay one rice paper wrapper into the water, turning over once, until softened (about six seconds). Then transfer to a work surface lined with paper towel.

- Fill the softened wrapper with a ¼ of the chicken filling. Fold down the ends, then roll. Lay seem-side-down on a serving plate spread with 1 cup field greens.

- Repeat the last two steps until all the filling and wrappers are used.

- Serve two per plate with a side of dipping sauce.

PHASE ① ...
TIME FOR SNACKS!

Chamomile Poached Pear

PREP TIME: 5 MIN, TOTAL TIME: 25 MIN

Chamomile tea is caffeine free and adds an herbal, earthly flavor to this pear that almost makes your snack feel like dessert. You can make a larger batch of these and store them in a jar in the refrigerator with their juices for up to a week.

- ✓ 1 ripe fresh pear, peeled, cored, and halved
- ✓ 1 cup strong-brewed chamomile tea
- ✓ 1 packet pure stevia extract (optional)
- ✓ 1 small strip lemon rind

- Bring all ingredients to a simmer in a small pot. Reduce heat and simmer on low for about 15 – 20 minutes or until the pear is tender. Remove to a dish with a slotted spoon, cover with remaining juices (optional) and serve cooled.

Chili-Lime Grilled Peach

Chili-Lime Grilled Peach

PREP TIME: 3 MIN,   TOTAL TIME: 10 MIN

There is nothing quite like the taste of a fresh, ripe peach. By grilling it, you bring those sweet undertones to the forefront and the chili and lime in this recipe give it a nice balance.

- ✓ 1 fresh peach
- ✓ ¼ tsp ground chili pepper
- ✓ Juice of ¼ lime

- Wash the peach and cut around the center from stem, to base, and back to stem. Twist to open and remove pit. Squeeze the lime juice to cover the cut flesh of the peach and sprinkle evenly with the chili pepper.

- Lay flat on a preheated grill (high heat) for about two minutes until the peach is juicy and char marks appear on the fruit. Serve hot.

Savory Kumquat and Scallion Salad

PREP TIME: 5 MIN, TOTAL TIME: 5 MIN

Kumquats are a sweet and sour fruit that have a slightly grainy texture and are delicious with savory dishes. If you like the crunch, you can leave the same in.

- ✓ 1 cup kumquats, seeded and sliced into 1/8" pieces
- ✓ 1 scallion (green onion), trimmed and thinly sliced
- ✓ ½ tsp white vinegar
- ✓ 1 tsp lemon juice
- ✓ ½ tsp sweet paprika
- ✓ ¼ tsp dry mustard
- ✓ Salt and cracked black pepper to taste

- Whisk together the lemon juice, vinegar, paprika, mustard, salt and pepper. Toss together with the kumquats and green onion and serve.

Minted Melon Sorbet

Fresh mint is the perfect complement for the sweet honey flavor that gives Honeydew melon its name. This sorbet is cool and refreshing and comes together in minutes. If you don't have an ice cream maker, freeze the melon chunks the night before and put the ingredients in your blender or food processor with a splash of water to get things moving.

- ✓ 1 ½ cups fresh Honeydew melon
- ✓ 3 fresh mint leaves
- ✓ Birch xylitol to taste (optional)

- Place all ingredients into the blender or food processor and blend until smooth. Pour into your frozen ice cream maker bowl and freeze according to manufacturer directions. Serve cold garnished with a mint leaf.

Cold Chocolate Cherry Soup

Cold Chocolate Cherry Soup

PREP TIME: 2 MIN,   TOTAL TIME: 5 MIN

This chilled soup tastes like a chocolate covered cherry and will sooth your sweet-tooth cravings. Raw cacao powder has a host of benefits including a healthy dose of magnesium, iron, vitamin B12, and properties that help control blood pressure. So, indulge with no guilt!

- ✓ 1 cup fresh or frozen (thawed) dark sweet cherries, pitted
- ✓ ¾ cup pure filtered water
- ✓ 1 tbsp raw cacao powder
- ✓ ½ tsp vanilla extract
- ✓ 1 -2 tsp birch xylitol (or to taste)
- ✓ Dash of ground cinnamon

- Place all ingredients in a food processor or high powered blender and process until smooth. Serve chilled.

PHASE ② ... BREAKFAST!

Minced Egg and Veggie Cucumber Boats

PREP TIME: 5 MIN,   TOTAL TIME: 5 MIN

This breakfast boat helps you clean up your leftovers, comes together quickly and can be eaten with your hands! Season with any Phase 2 herbs and spices that compliment your leftovers. Try some fresh parsley or cilantro with a squeeze of lime, or Bragg Liquid Aminos with garlic and ginger.

- ✓ 1 large cucumber
- ✓ 1 cup minced leftover Phase 2 vegetables
- ✓ 3 egg whites, chopped
- ✓ Seasoning to taste

- • Wash the cucumber and peel it in stripes, leaving some peel on for the fiber and nutrients (or do not peel). With a metal spoon, scoop out the center to about ½" or just enough to get the seeds out.

- • Mix the chopped egg with finely chopped or minced leftover cooked or raw veggies. Try it with stir-fried bell peppers, mushrooms, shallots, and garlic!

Brussels Sprouts, Bacon, and Mushroom Grill

Brussels Sprouts, Bacon, and Mushroom Grill

PREP TIME: 5 MIN, TOTAL TIME: 15 MIN

Brussels sprouts have the flavor profile of a mini cabbage and are delicious with the smokiness of bacon and a bit of earthiness from the mushrooms. Shallot taste like a mild blend of garlic and onion, without the aftertaste that usually accompanies their more powerful cousins. If peeling these tiny bulbs is too time consuming, you can usually find them peeled in your grocer's produce section.

- ✓ 4 slices turkey bacon
- ✓ 1 cup Brussels sprouts, trimmed and halved
- ✓ ½ cup shallots, peeled and trimmed
- ✓ ½ cup button mushrooms, cleaned
- ✓ 1 tbsp fresh, chopped lemon thyme
- ✓ Sea salt and cracked black pepper

- Cut the turkey bacon into 2" pieces. Toss the cut sprouts, bacon, and shallots into a large nonstick skillet and cook for about five minutes, stirring to make sure everything gets coated with the little bit of fat provided by the turkey bacon.

- When the bacon is starting to brown and the sprouts are fragrant, add the mushrooms. Cook about three minutes until the mushrooms are softened. Add the lemon thyme, salt and pepper to taste. Turn to coat and warm through. Serve immediately.

Reuben Hash with Mustard Greens

PREP TIME: 5 MIN,   TOTAL TIME: 15 MIN

This dish combines all the wonderful flavors of a classic Reuben sandwich in just one pan. Sauerkraut, a staple of the Reuben, is simply cabbage fermented with salt and is a fantastic gut healer, making this breakfast great if you are feeling a bit bloated.

- ✓ 4 oz corned beef deli slices (precooked)
- ✓ 1 cup natural sauerkraut
- ✓ ½ cup finely sliced yellow onion
- ✓ 1 cup fresh mustard greens
- ✓ ¼ cup beef stock
- ✓ 1 tsp birch xylitol
- ✓ ¼ tsp mustard seeds
- ✓ Pinch of red pepper flakes
- ✓ Sea salt and pepper to taste

- Place the onion in a large nonstick pan with the beef stock and xylitol. Bring to a simmer, stirring frequently, until the onion is becoming translucent (about three minutes).

- Add the sauerkraut and beef and cook until heated through. The broth will begin to simmer off and the pan will get a bit dry. This is good because you want your dish to begin to brown a bit.

- Once the onion and kraut are beginning to brown, add the mustard greens, mustard seeds, pepper flakes, salt and pepper and turn gently. Cook for a few minutes until the greens are wilted and flavors are nicely blended, (about three minutes). Serve hot off the griddle.

Jicama and Dilled Salmon Stacks [serves 2]

PREP TIME: 10 MIN, TOTAL TIME: 10 MIN

This is a quick, light breakfast that comes together in just minutes without any cooking at all. The crisp jicama provides the platform for the rich, smoky salmon. Look for medium-sized jicama bulbs, about the size of your fist. If the jicama gets too large, it will start to taste too starchy and woody.

- ✓ 1 medium jicama bulb
- ✓ 6 oz smoked salmon (Lox)
- ✓ ½ red onion, peeled and finely minced
- ✓ ¼ cup fresh dill weed
- ✓ ½ cup watercress
- ✓ 1 lemon wedge
- ✓ Cracked black pepper

- Peel the jicama and slice into very thin rounds. You can use only the larger rounds, saving the smaller pieces for a salad later on.

- Divide the lox evenly between the jicama slices.

- Top with watercress, dill weed, and minced onion. Drizzle with the juice from the lemon wedge and top with cracked black pepper.

Beef and Bell Pepper Skillet

Beef and Bell Pepper Skillet

This quick skillet breakfast is even faster with leftover steak or roast from the night before! Rare-cooked tenderloin or sirloin steaks work well in this recipe. If you want to bulk it up with more veggies, serve it over a bed of fresh mixed greens.

- ✓ 4 oz lean beef, thinly sliced
- ✓ 1 green bell pepper, trimmed and sliced
- ✓ 1 red bell pepper, trimmed and sliced
- ✓ ½ red onion, peeled, trimmed, and sliced into thin rings
- ✓ 1 – 2 tsp tamari or Bragg's liquid aminos
- ✓ Cracked black pepper to taste

- • Heat all ingredients in a medium nonstick skillet set over medium-low heat until the beef is cooked to your liking and the peppers and onion are crisp-tender. Stir regularly. Serve piping hot!

Green Latkes with Crumbled Bacon

Latkes are a traditional Jewish potato pancake made of shredded potato, onion, and flour and fried in oil. While these shredded green cakes resemble the Dr. Seuss "Green Eggs and Ham" version of latkes, they taste nothing like their potato cousin. The hearty, nutty broccoli gets a cheesy flavor from the nutritional yeast and a smoky crunch from the turkey bacon.

- ✓ 2 cups broccoli slaw (shredded broccoli)
- ✓ 2 green onions, thinly sliced
- ✓ 1 slice turkey bacon
- ✓ 3 egg whites

- ✓ 1 tbsp arrowroot starch
- ✓ 1 tbsp nutritional yeast flakes
- ✓ 1 tsp prepared whole grain mustard
- ✓ Sea salt and ground black pepper to taste

- Place the broccoli slaw in a microwave safe bowl with ½ cup water. Cover tightly with plastic wrap and microwave on high for three to five minutes. Let sit, covered, in the microwave about a minute to cool to the touch before removing with caution. Carefully peel back the plastic wrap and drain out the water.

- To the slaw, add the green onions, arrowroot starch, nutritional yeast flakes, mustard, salt and pepper and turn to completely coat. Add the egg whites and mix thoroughly. Set aside.

- Lay the bacon in the bottom of a nonstick pan set over medium-high heat. Cook about 90 seconds on each side until crisp. Remove to a cutting board and chop into bits.

- Form the green latkes into three or four small patties. Wet your hands if necessary to prevent sticking.

- Lay the patties in the pan from which you removed the bacon. Cook for about two minutes, or until crisp on one side. Flip and continue cooking until both sides are crisp and the center is set.

- Remove latkes to a serving plate and top with bacon bits.

Sweet Jicama Cobbler

PREP TIME: 5 MIN,   TOTAL TIME: 40 MIN

Sometimes you just want a little something sweet with your morning tea, and this jicama crisp takes the cake. Jicama has a slightly sweet flavor that hints of apples, with a similar texture. When you wrap it in the spices of an apple pie, you almost can't tell the difference!

- ✓ 1 ¾ cups peeled and thinly sliced jicama
- ✓ ¼ cup arrowroot powder
- ✓ 3 tbsp birch xylitol
- ✓ Juice from ½ lemon
- ✓ ½ tsp each: cinnamon, nutmeg, vanilla extract

- Make sure your jicama is very thinly sliced, and cut into about 1 ½ - 2" pieces. They should be about the shape and size of thinly sliced apples for pie-making.

- Preheat oven to 350°F.

- Place all ingredients in a large mixing bowl and mix until evenly coated.

- Pour batter into a small casserole dish or 7" ceramic individual ramekin.

- Bake in the preheated oven for 25 – 30 minutes or until the jicama is tender and the cobbler is set. It should be golden brown on top.

- Sprinkle with cinnamon (optional) and serve.

PHASE ②... LUNCH TIME!

Warm Green Beans, Shallots & Bacon

PREP TIME: 5 MIN, TOTAL TIME: 15 MIN

This is a simple, one-pan meal that is warm and filling. The smokiness of the bacon, the garlic-onion flavor of the shallots, and the earthy green beans work well together to create a dish that can be a meal all in itself or a side dish with your dinner.

- ✓ 1 ½ cups fresh green beans
- ✓ 5 strips turkey bacon
- ✓ 4 shallots, peeled and halved
- ✓ 1/3 cup chicken stock
- ✓ ½ tsp red pepper flakes (or to taste)
- ✓ ½ tsp sea salt

- Cook the bacon in a large skillet over medium heat until it's browned and crisp on one side, (or about two minutes). Flip and crisp the other side. Remove to a plate.

- Add the chicken stock, green beans and shallots into the skillet. Bring to a simmer, turning with a spatula occasionally. Simmer for about five minutes, or until the beans are tender and the stock is reduced. Season with red pepper flakes and sea salt.

- Drain any remaining liquid. Place the beans and shallots on a plate. Cut the bacon into 2" pieces and place them on top of the beans. Serve immediately.

Dilled Jicama "Potato Salad"

Dilled Jicama "Potato Salad"

This potato salad will make you reminisce of summer picnics. With the jicama, there is no boiling required. Its tender-crisp mildness takes on the flavors of the dressing and vegetables. Egg whites add a protein that's common in traditional potato salad.

- ✓ 2 cups peeled and cubed jicama
- ✓ ¼ cup red onion, diced
- ✓ ¼ cup celery, diced
- ✓ 1 dill pickle, diced
- ✓ 1 tbsp fresh dill weed, chopped
- ✓ 2 tbsp coconut vinegar
- ✓ ½ tsp each dry mustard, sea salt, black pepper
- ✓ ½ tsp birch xylitol
- ✓ Whites from three boiled eggs, chopped

- In a small bowl, whisk together the coconut vinegar, mustard, salt, pepper, and xylitol. Stir in the dill weed.

- Peel and cube the jicama into 1" cubes (or smaller) and place in a large bowl. Add the red onion, celery, and dill pickle. Mix in the dressing to coat. Gently mix in the egg whites. Serve chilled.

French Onion Soup with Crisp Jicama Chips

French Onion Soup may seem like a decadent meal that takes a lot of work, but it's actually quite simple. The preparation is easy, it just takes time to simmer the delicious sugars out of the onion and into the broth. Serve it with crunchy jicama chips instead of a crouton, and you will not walk away from lunch hungry!

- ✓ 1 large Vidalia onion
- ✓ 4 oz lean beef, finely sliced
- ✓ 1 small jicama bulb
- ✓ 2 cups beef stock
- ✓ 1 tsp arrowroot starch
- ✓ ½ tsp birch xylitol
- ✓ ½ tsp each chili powder, sea salt, and white pepper

- Peel, trim and slice the onion into thick rings. Place the onions and beef in a large pan and sprinkle with the xylitol and arrowroot starch. Pour in the beef stock and bring to a simmer over high heat. Reduce heat, place a lid on the pan, and simmer for about 45 minutes or until the onions are tender and the broth has thickened.

- Preheat the oven to 400°F. Peel the jicama and slice very thin with a sharp knife or mandolin. Set a metal bakery rack on top of a baking sheet. Lay the jicama slices in a single layer on the rack and sprinkle with the chili powder, sea salt, and white pepper mixture. Bake for about 45 minutes or until the chips are golden and crisp.

- Pour the soup into a bowl and serve with the crisp jicama chips on the side, or sprinkle them on top of the soup for a nice crunch that replaces the traditional crouton.

Green & Garlicky Pesto Chicken Lettuce Cups

With a bit of leftover chicken on hand, this lunch comes together in minutes and is a hearty, satisfying meal. The "pesto" flavors of basil and garlic are mimicked in this sauce that is free of the oils or pine nuts traditionally found in pesto.

- ✓ 4 oz roasted or grilled chicken breast
- ✓ ½ cup baby spinach, chopped
- ✓ 2 tbsp chopped fresh basil
- ✓ 1 clove minced garlic
- ✓ 1 tsp nutritional yeast flakes
- ✓ 1 tsp lemon juice
- ✓ 1 tsp water
- ✓ ½ tsp stone ground mustard
- ✓ Pinch of sea salt and pepper
- ✓ 4 - 5 leaves of butter lettuce (cups)

- In a small bowl, whisk together the lemon juice, water, mustard, and nutritional yeast flakes. Add the garlic, basil, salt and pepper and stir until well-mixed.

- Chop or shred the chicken breast, then mix it with the pesto dressing until completely coated.

- Fill each lettuce cup evenly and top with a sprinkling of the shredded spinach.

Spicy Buffalo and Chili Stuffed Peppers

Spicy Buffalo and Chili Stuffed Peppers

PREP TIME: 15 MIN, TOTAL TIME: 75 MIN

If you like a little kick to your lunch, these stuffed peppers will fulfill your spiciest desires. The egg whites hold everything together to make a kind of southwestern meatloaf stuffed into a cool red pepper.

- ✓ 4 oz ground buffalo
- ✓ 1 red bell pepper
- ✓ 1 jalapeno, seeded
- ✓ 1 clove garlic, peeled
- ✓ ¼ of a white onion
- ✓ 1 cup packed baby spinach
- ✓ 2 egg whites, beaten

- ✓ ½ tsp cumin
- ✓ ½ tsp chili powder
- ✓ ½ tsp dried oregano
- ✓ Sea salt and pepper to taste
- ✓ Squirt of Tabasco and 1 tbsp chopped cilantro (optional, for serving)

- Preheat oven to 350°F. Wash the bell pepper and cut it lengthwise from stem to base. Remove the seeds and lay open in a shallow baking dish.

- Place the jalapeno, garlic, and onion into a food processor. Pulse until the vegetables are finely chopped. Add the spinach and pulse again, until the mixture resembles a pesto.

- Place the ground buffalo in a large glass bowl. Add the processed vegetables and remaining spices. Using your clean hands, mix everything together. Add the egg whites and mix again until everything sticks together. Stuff half of the meat mixture into each half of the bell pepper. Bake in the preheated oven for about 45 minutes, or until a meat thermometer inserted into the center reads 175°F. Allow to rest about ten minutes before topping with Tabasco and cilantro (optional) for serving.

Egg Drop Soup and Chinese Cabbage Salad

Egg Drop Soup is one of those typical carry-out items that is rarely made at home, but there's no reason not to. It's really quite simple. Take your time threading the eggs into the broth, but don't worry. Even if you don't end up with perfect egg threads, it will still taste phenomenal.

For the soup

- ✓ 1 ½ cups chicken broth
- ✓ 2 tsp arrowroot starch, divided
- ✓ 1 ½ tsp tamari
- ✓ Pinch red pepper flakes (or to taste)
- ✓ 3 egg whites, beaten

For the salad

- ✓ 1 cup Napa cabbage, shredded
- ✓ 2 radishes, trimmed and quartered
- ✓ 1 green onion, sliced
- ✓ ½ small cucumber, sliced

- ✓ 1 tbsp coconut vinegar
- ✓ ½ tbsp. tamari
- ✓ Juice of one lemon wedge
- ✓ ½ tsp prepared horseradish

- *To make the salad:* Plate the cabbage and top with radishes, onion, and cucumber. In a small bowl, whisk together the vinegar, tamari, horseradish, and juice from the lemon wedge. Pour over the plated vegetables and serve chilled.

- *To make the soup:* Beat the egg whites with 1 tablespoon arrowroot starch. In a small saucepan set over medium heat, whisk together the chicken broth, 1 tsp arrowroot powder, tamari and pepper flakes (optional). Bring to a boil. Using a spoon, stir the broth in one direction to create a swirl. Slowly drizzle in the egg whites over the back of a fork to separate. Keep swirling, breaking up the eggs as you pour them in. Continue to cook, stirring, about one minute after all the egg has been added. Serve hot with the salad on the side.

Mixed Grill Salad with Fennel & Smoked Salmon

PREP TIME: 15 MIN, TOTAL TIME: 25 MIN

Even if your grill is covered in a foot of snow, or if you don't have one, you can make this dish using your oven's broiler. Just place the cut vegetables on a rimmed baking sheet and broil until charred. Flip and broil the other side. You'll get that grilled taste without going outside!

- ✓ 1 fennel bulb
- ✓ 3 spears asparagus
- ✓ 1 red bell pepper
- ✓ ½ red onion
- ✓ Romaine heart
- ✓ 4 oz smoked salmon slices
- ✓ 2 tbsp cider vinegar
- ✓ 1 tbsp lemon juice
- ✓ 1 tbsp water
- ✓ 1 tsp birch xylitol
- ✓ 1 tsp stone ground garlic mustard
- ✓ Salt and black pepper

- Whisk together the cider vinegar, lemon juice, water, xylitol, mustard, salt and pepper. Set aside. Preheat your gas, electric, or charcoal grill to high heat.

- Trim the fennel bulb and cut it into about eight wedges. Wash and trim the asparagus and cut into three pieces each. Trim the onion and cut into wedges. Seed and trim the bell pepper and cut into eight wedges. Toss the cut vegetables in ½ of the dressing mixture to lightly coat. Place in a vegetable grill basket and grill over high heat until one side begins to char, (about two minutes). Flip and slightly char the other side.

- Slice the romaine heart in half and top with the grilled vegetables, salmon, and the remaining dressing. Serve immediately.

PHASE ②... DINNER IS SERVED!

Grilled Ahi Tuna and Romaine Hearts

PREP TIME: 15 MIN, TOTAL TIME: 20 MIN

The grill is perfect for quick meals with minimal cleanup, and this Ahi tuna and Romaine dinner is just that. Its flavors are so complex and delicate that anyone would be surprised at how simple it is to make.

- ✓ 1 4oz Ahi Tuna steak
- ✓ 1 Romaine lettuce heart (a head with the loose leafy greens removed)
- ✓ 1 tbsp finely minced red onion
- ✓ ¼ cup thinly sliced cucumber
- ✓ 1 tsp very coarsely ground black pepper
- ✓ ½ tsp coarse sea salt or kosher salt

For Ginger-Lime Vinaigrette:

- ✓ ¼ cup coconut vinegar (or cider vinegar)
- ✓ 1 tbsp fresh lime juice
- ✓ ½ tsp freshly grated ginger
- ✓ 2 drops liquid stevia extract

- Preheat a gas, electric, or charcoal grill to high heat. Prepare the Ginger-Lime Vinaigrette by whisking together the vinegar, lime juice, grated ginger, and stevia. Set aside.

- Wash and dry the Romaine heart. Slice vertically to split the lettuce down the center, keeping the leaves intact by the root. Brush the cut side with the vinaigrette, saving any remaining dressing to drizzle after grilling.

- Coat the tuna steak with the cracked black pepper and salt. Place the tuna and Romaine hearts (cut side down) on the preheated grill. Cook the tuna for about 1 ½ minutes on each side for rare, or cook longer for desired doneness. Cook the Romaine hearts about 2 – 3 minutes until the cut side begins to char. Do not flip.

- Plate the grilled lettuce cut side up and top with onion, cucumber, and remaining dressing. Serve alongside the peppered tuna steak.

Venison Stew with Shallots & Radish

Venison Stew with Shallots & Radish [serves 4]

PREP TIME: 20 MIN,   TOTAL TIME: 75 MIN

Venison is a very lean, gamey meat that is similar in texture to beef. It is perfect for roasts, stews, and even mixed with other meats to make sausages and burgers. The flavors of the radish and shallots compliment the meat to create a nicely spiced, hearty meal for a cold day.

- ✓ 1 ½ lb venison stew meat, cut into 1" cubes
- ✓ 4 slices turkey bacon
- ✓ 2 cups whole shallots, peeled
- ✓ 1 lb radishes, washed, trimmed and halved
- ✓ 4 celery stalks, trimmed and sliced
- ✓ 1 lb fresh mustard greens, washed, trimmed and coarsely chopped
- ✓ 4 cups organic beef broth

- ✓ 2 bay leaves
- ✓ ¼ cup red wine vinegar
- ✓ 3 tbsp arrowroot starch
- ✓ 1 tbsp fresh chopped thyme
- ✓ 1 tbsp fresh chopped basil
- ✓ 1 tsp smoked paprika
- ✓ ½ tsp dried oregano
- ✓ 1 tsp sea salt
- ✓ 1 tsp ground black pepper

- In a large pan with a lid, or a Dutch oven, fry the turkey bacon until crisp. Remove to a plate and set aside, but leave the pan over the heat. Mix together the arrowroot starch, paprika, oregano, sea salt, and black pepper.

- Toss the venison in the arrowroot mixture to coat. Sear it in the heated pan for about 2 – 3 minutes. Add the onion and cook about two minutes, stirring regularly. Add the celery and radish, cook another few minutes. Deglaze the pan with the red wine vinegar.

- Add the beef stock, bay leaves, thyme and basil. Stir and bring to a boil. Stir again and reduce to a simmer. Cover and let simmer 45 minutes. The sauce should be slightly thickened. Add the mustard greens, stir, replace the lid and continue simmering another five minutes until the meat is tender and the greens are wilted but not mushy. Serve hot.

Chicken & Cremini Enchiladas Florentine [serves 2]

PREP TIME: 15 MIN, TOTAL TIME: 25 MIN

This meal takes a bit of time to prepare, but is well worth it. Nutritional yeast flakes mimic the creaminess of the sauce typically found in Florentine dishes, and the green chilies give these enchiladas a spicy kick. You can make a double batch of the egg white tortillas and refrigerate them for a quick roll-up when you need a protein snack.

- ✓ 4 oz leftover roasted or grilled chicken, shredded
- ✓ 4 egg whites, separated
- ✓ 2 slices turkey bacon
- ✓ 1 ½ cups diced Cremini mushrooms
- ✓ 1/2 cup diced white onion
- ✓ 2 cups fresh baby spinach, shredded
- ✓ ½ cup diced green chilies
- ✓ 1 cup nutritional yeast flakes
- ✓ 2 cups chicken broth
- ✓ 5 tsp arrowroot starch
- ✓ 1 clove garlic, crushed
- ✓ 1 tsp dry mustard
- ✓ Sea salt to taste
- ✓ ¼ cup chopped fresh cilantro

- To make the egg white tortillas: Whip the four egg whites together with one tablespoon of water. In a large nonstick skillet, cook the turkey bacon until crisp, flip and cook the other side. Remove to a plate.

- Using the same skillet, pour out half of the egg whites into a large, thin circle. Cook until the egg white bubbles and the bottom is browning, about one minute. Flip and cook the other side for about thirty seconds. Remove to a plate and repeat with the other half of the egg mixture. Set aside.

- To make the creamy filling and sauce: In a sauce pot, whisk together the chicken broth, nutritional yeast flakes, arrowroot starch, and dry mustard, sea salt and pepper over medium heat. Continue cooking and whisking until the sauce thickens. Add in the chicken, spinach, onion, and green chilies and stir. Cook just until heat through.

- Scoop about ½ cup of the sauce into the bottom of an oven-proof dish (like a glass pie pan). Try to leave more of the chunks behind in the pot. Fill the two egg white "tortillas" with as much of the filling as possible while still being able to roll the enchilada. Use a slotted spoon to get the filling out so you get more chunks, leaving more of the sauce behind. Roll each enchilada and place in the pie pan with the ends facing down.

- Pour remaining sauce over the enchiladas and broil on high for about three minutes until the sauce is brown and bubbly. While it's broiling, chop the turkey bacon into small bits.

- Plate one enchilada and half of the sauce on each of two plates. Top with half of the turkey bacon and chopped fresh cilantro and serve hot.

Minted Lamb Chops & Kale

Minted Lamb Chops & Kale [serves 4]

Don't be afraid of cooking lamb chops! While they truly are a delicacy, they are also simple to prepare... The key is choosing the right chops. You'll want to find lamb chops with pink meat, bright white fat, and dark pink bones. Use fresh, not frozen. Developing a good relationship with your local butcher is a fantastic way to get the meat you're looking for. And as always, choose hormone-free, local meat whenever possible.

Lamb Chops:

- ✓ 8 lamb loin chops (about 5 oz each, trimmed)
- ✓ ¼ cup chicken or vegetable broth
- ✓ 1/3 cup fresh mint leaves, coarsely chopped

- ✓ 4 garlic cloves, crushed
- ✓ 1 tsp ground cumin
- ✓ 1 tsp ground cayenne pepper
- ✓ 1 tsp ground black pepper
- ✓ Lemon wedges

Garlic Kale:

- ✓ 2 pounds tender kale, trimmed
- ✓ 2 cloves garlic, minced
- ✓ ½ cup plus one tablespoon vegetable stock

- ✓ 2 tbsp red wine vinegar
- ✓ Salt and black pepper to taste

- To make the kale: Add one tablespoon of stock and the garlic to a large pan set over medium heat. Cook the garlic, stirring, for about two minutes or until it is soft and fragrant. Add the remaining stock and kale, turning to coat. Increase to high heat and cook, covered for about five minutes. Remove lid, stir, and cook uncovered until all the liquid is evaporated. Drizzle with red wine vinegar, salt and pepper to taste.

- To make the chops: Mix together the broth, cumin, cayenne, black pepper, garlic, and half of the mint leaves. Spread the herb mixture over both sides of the chops and lay in a broiling pan to rest about ten minutes. Broil 3 ½ - 5 minutes on each side until the meat is brown and crisp. Remove to serving plates and sprinkle with remaining chopped mint leaves and a squeeze of lemon juice. Serve with sautéed kale.

Pork Tenderloin with Rhubarb Compote [serves 4]

PREP: 15 MIN, TOTAL TIME: 1 HOUR

This is a perfect dish to prepare for your family or when you're having dinner guests. Prepare the meat and get it in the oven, then start the compote when you are resting the tenderloin. This way, everything comes together at the same time. The sweet rhubarb compote balances the salty-savory pork for a meal that will earn you culinary praise!

Tenderloin:

- ✓ 2 lb pork tenderloin
- ✓ 2 garlic cloves, crushed
- ✓ 1 tbsp fresh thyme, finely chopped
- ✓ 1 tsp cracked black pepper
- ✓ 1 tsp sea salt

Compote:

- ✓ 2 lbs fresh rhubarb
- ✓ ¾ cup birch xylitol
- ✓ 1 tbsp lemon juice

- Preheat oven to 350°F. Mix together the garlic, thyme, salt and pepper. Using your clean hands, rub the spice mixture into the tenderloin so that it sticks. Make sure it's completely covered in seasoning. Place the seasoned tenderloin in a shallow baking dish and bake in preheated oven for about 45 – 60 minutes or until a meat thermometer reads 150°F. Let the tenderloin rest, covered, about ten minutes before slicing.

- To make the compote, trim the ends from the rhubarb and slice on a diagonal into ¾" pieces. Place the rhubarb in a large bowl and toss it with the xylitol. Pour into a heavy saucepan set over medium heat. Stir in the lemon juice. Bring to a boil. Reduce to a simmer and cook, stirring often, for about five minutes until rhubarb is completely soft and sauce has thickened.

- Slice the tenderloin and divide it evenly between four dinner plates. Top with the warm rhubarb compote.

Steamed Gingered Cod and Asparagus [serves 2]

PREP TIME: 5 MIN, TOTAL: 15 MIN

This fish dish has an Asian flare and comes together quickly in one pot. Prep and cleanup are both a breeze. If your cod filets are frozen, make sure to defrost them overnight in the refrigerator. Other types of whitefish will also work in a pinch!

- ✓ 2 6oz skinless cod filets
- ✓ 12 – 16 asparagus spears, fibrous ends trimmed off
- ✓ 6 green onions
- ✓ 2 tbsp white wine vinegar
- ✓ 1 tbsp liquid coconut aminos
- ✓ 1 tbsp finely grated fresh ginger
- ✓ Coarse sea salt and cracked black pepper
- ✓ 2 lemon wedges

- In a medium pan, whisk together the white wine vinegar, coconut aminos, and fresh ginger. Season the fish on both sides with sea salt and black pepper and lay them into the pan. Bring to a boil, cover and reduce to a simmer. Cook for about 6 – 8 minutes until fish is almost opaque.

- While fish is cooking, trim the green onion and slice the dark green portions vertically down the center, making long strips. Cut those strips into three-inch lengths. Lay the onion strips on top of the fish, then lay the asparagus over top of that.

- Cover and continue cooking for an additional three to five minutes until asparagus are tender-crisp. Serve hot with a lemon wedge.

Smoky Chicken Kebabs & Romaine [serves 2]

Just because you can't have sweet and tangy, drippy barbeque sauce doesn't mean you can't enjoy all the flavors! By tossing chicken cubes in a combination of spices, liquid smoke, and vinegar, these quick and easy bite-sized chicken kebabs are a snap on the grill. Throw some halved Romaine heads right on next to them and your meal is complete.

- ✓ 8 ounces boneless, skinless chicken breast
- ✓ 2 small Romaine hearts

For the chicken marinade:

- ✓ 1 ½ tbsp cider vinegar
- ✓ 1 tsp liquid smoke
- ✓ 3 drops liquid stevia extract
- ✓ 1 tsp chili powder
- ✓ 1 tsp paprika
- ✓ ½ tsp chipotle powder
- ✓ ¼ tsp cinnamon

For the Romaine dressing:

- ✓ Juice of one lemon
- ✓ 1 tbsp balsamic vinegar
- ✓ 1 drop liquid stevia
- ✓ ½ tsp dried turmeric
- ✓ ½ tsp sea salt
- ✓ Cracked white pepper to taste

- Place four bamboo skewers into a pan of water to soak for about fifteen minutes to prevent charring.

- Cut the chicken breast into 1" cubes and place them into a large zip-top plastic storage bag.

- Whisk together the marinade ingredients and pour into the bag with the chicken. Toss to completely coat. At this point, you can either let the chicken marinade in the refrigerator for several hours to overnight, or proceed straight to the next step.

- Whisk together the Romaine dressing ingredients.

- Pull any loose leaves off of the Romaine hearts. Cut the Romaine hearts horizontally down the center, keeping each half intact. Using a kitchen brush, apply a thin coat of the dressing to the cut sides of the Romaine hearts.

- Thread the chicken onto the soaked bamboo skewers, leaving about half of the skewer for turning.

- Place the chicken skewers and the flat sides of the Romaine hearts onto the grill. Remove the Romaine in about two minutes, when the cut side is starting to char.

- Turn the kebabs every two minutes until each side is done and the juices run clear. Remove to serving plates. Add the grilled Romaine and drizzle with any remaining dressing.

PHASE ②...
TIME FOR SNACKS!

Pizza Puffs [serves 2]

PREP TIME: 5 MIN,   TOTAL TIME: 90 MIN

These little puffs have the flavors of a cheese pizza with the texture of a cheese puff! Essentially, you are making a light, airy, savory merengue perfect for snacking on during a movie or any time. Since they take a little while to bake and cool, make them on the second day of Phase 1 so you have them ready when you're hungry in Phase 2.

- ✓ ½ cup liquid egg whites
- ✓ 2 tsp nutritional yeast flakes
- ✓ ¼ tsp dried basil flakes
- ✓ ¼ tsp dried oregano flakes
- ✓ ¼ tsp ground mustard powder
- ✓ ½ tsp paprika

- Preheat oven to 200°F. Place the egg whites into the bowl of a kitchen mixer. Beat on high for about three minutes until stiff peaks form. Using a rubber spatula, gently fold in the nutritional yeast flakes and spices.

- Line a baking sheet with parchment paper. Drop the egg white mixture onto the paper by the teaspoonful, or use a pastry bag to pipe the mixture onto the paper. Bake in the preheated oven for one hour. Turn off the heat and let the puffs rest in the oven for another hour.

Beef-Wrapped Spicy Pickles

Beef-Wrapped Spicy Pickles

PREP TIME: 5 MIN, TOTAL TIME: 5 MIN

Deli slices are good to have on hand for quick snacking during this phase. Most health food groceries and some regular supermarkets will carry the nitrite-free, hormone-free varieties.

- ✓ 3 slices nitrite-free deli roast beef
- ✓ 3 pickle spears (no sugar added)
- ✓ ½ tsp cayenne pepper

- Lay the roast beef slices on a clean work surface. Place a pickle spear on the edge of each beef slice. Sprinkle each with 1/3 of the cayenne pepper. Roll the pickle up in the beef and enjoy!

Ginger Tamari Salmon Jerky [serves 4]

PREP TIME: Over Night,   TOTAL TIME: 18 HOURS

Salmon jerky is a delicious alternative to beef. By dehydrating the salmon, you get rid of a lot of the fat just as you would by smoking it. Make a batch of this during Phase 1 so you have it on hand when you need it!

- ✓ 1 lb fresh wild caught salmon
- ✓ ¼ cup tamari
- ✓ 2 cloves garlic, crushed
- ✓ 2 tsp grated fresh ginger
- ✓ 1 tsp lemon juice

- Remove the skin and fat from the salmon. Slice the fish into very thin, long slices. Place it into a large zip-top plastic bag. Add in the tamari, garlic, ginger, and lemon juice. Shake to coat and refrigerate six hours or overnight.

- Preheat oven to 185°F. Spread the marinated salmon on a wire baking rack set over top a rimmed baking sheet. Bake for 6 – 8 hours, flipping half way through, until the jerky breaks when you bend it.

Chicken Bites with Smoky Green Chile Dip

PREP TIME: 5 MIN, TOTAL TIME: 5 MIN

It's always a good idea to cook extra meat for your lunches and dinners. Refrigerate or freeze the leftovers for snacking or quick lunches later in the week. If you don't have any leftovers on hand for this snack, simply cut a raw chicken breast into cubes and thread onto three skewers, leaving a bit of space between. Broil for about three minutes on each side.

- ✓ 4 oz leftover chicken breast, grilled or baked
- ✓ 1 green chili, seeded
- ✓ 2 cloves garlic
- ✓ 2 tbsp coconut vinegar
- ✓ 1 tbsp lemon juice
- ✓ 2 tsp birch xylitol
- ✓ 1 tsp sea salt
- ✓ 1 tsp ground cumin
- ✓ ½ tsp liquid smoke
- ✓ Tabasco to taste (optional)

- Cut the chicken into bite-sized cubes. Place remaining ingredients into a high-powered blender or food processor and blend until smooth. Serve the bites alongside the dip.

Tuna Stuffed Egg Whites

Tuna Stuffed Egg Whites

Boiled eggs are a good thing to have on hand during any phase of this diet. Slice down the center and discard the yolk, saving the whites for a quick protein snack or to use as a casing for this tuna-stuffed "deviled" egg.

- ✓ 3 oz water-packed canned tuna, drained
- ✓ 3 boiled eggs, white only, sliced in half
- ✓ 2 green onions, pale green and white parts only
- ✓ 2 tsp chopped fresh parsley
- ✓ Sea salt and cracked black pepper to taste

- Slice the boiled eggs in half lengthwise and discard the yolk. Very thinly slice the green onion.

- Mash together the tuna, green onion, parsley, sea salt and pepper.

- Stuff the tuna mixture into the egg whites.

- Serve chilled or at room temperature.

PHASE ③ ... BREAKFAST!

Black Bean Breakfast Burrito

Black beans are a nice change of pace after all the meat in Phase 2! You can spice up this dish with fresh jalapenos or red pepper flakes. If you don't want eggs, you can cut them out and add two tablespoons of guacamole before wrapping. This recipe is versatile and delicious.

- ✓ 1/3 cup canned black beans, drained
- ✓ 1 egg white, whisked
- ✓ 1 cup diced mixed peppers and onions
- ✓ 1 clove garlic, crushed
- ✓ 1 tsp olive oil
- ✓ ½ tsp cumin
- ✓ ½ tsp chili powder
- ✓ ½ tsp salt
- ✓ ½ cup fresh salsa (no sugar added)
- ✓ 1 sprouted grain tortilla
- ✓ 1 cup Phase 3 fruit

- Heat the oil in a medium nonstick pan. Add the onion and pepper blend and garlic. Cook, stirring, until onions and peppers are tender (about five minutes).

- Add beans, cumin, chili powder, and salt and stir to coat. Add egg white and cook, stirring with a rubber spatula, until eggs are cooked through.

- Pour the filling into a sprouted grain tortilla, top with salsa, and roll. Serve with a side of Phase 3 fruit.

Pumpkin Quinoa Griddle Cakes

Pumpkin Quinoa Griddle Cakes [Serves 4]

PREP TIME: 5 MIN, TOTAL TIME: 10 MIN

These rustic hotcakes are filled with the flavors of your grandmother's pumpkin pie. A serving size is three cakes, so make this recipe for your family or freeze the leftovers for a quick toaster meal next week.

Keep in mind that if you are using fresh pumpkin, about four cups of fresh pumpkin cubes (or a 4 pound pie pumpkin) will cook down and be pureed into about one cup of pumpkin puree.

You'll find baking powder on this ingredients list. Make sure that your baking powder is corn-free. Corn is a metabolic nightmare and should always be avoided.

- ✓ 1 cup cooked pureed pumpkin (fresh or canned)
- ✓ 1 cup plain rice milk
- ✓ 1 cup quinoa flour
- ✓ 2 eggs, beaten
- ✓ 3 tbsp raw almond butter
- ✓ 1 tbsp coconut oil
- ✓ 1 tsp pumpkin pie spice
- ✓ 1 tsp pure vanilla extract
- ✓ 1 tsp birch xylitol
- ✓ 1 tsp baking powder
- ✓ 4 cups Phase 3 fruit for serving

- Heat a nonstick griddle to medium-high. In a mixing bowl, whisk together the quinoa flour, pumpkin pie spice, birch xylitol, and baking powder. Add the pumpkin puree, rice milk, almond butter, and eggs, mixing thoroughly.

- Coat the griddle with coconut oil.

- Spoon the batter by the ¼-cupful onto the hot griddle. Cook until golden and crisp, flipping when the batter bubbles on top. Repeat until all the batter is used.

- Serve with 1 cup Phase 3 fruit.

Okra, Jicama, and Sausage Skillet

When you're choosing okra, make sure it's at its freshest to avoid the dreaded okra slime. Pick bright green, thumb-sized pieces and use within two days of purchasing fresh from a farmer's market, if possible. Do not use frozen okra for this dish.

- ✓ 1 cup fresh thumb-sized okra (about 6 – 8)
- ✓ 1 cup peeled and diced jicama
- ✓ 3 oz nitrate-free spicy chicken sausage
- ✓ 1 tbsp + ½ tsp olive oil, divided
- ✓ 2 cloves garlic, crushed
- ✓ ½ tsp crushed red pepper flakes
- ✓ 1 lemon wedge
- ✓ 1 slice sprouted grain bread
- ✓ Sea salt and pepper to taste
- ✓ 1 grapefruit

- Clean and dry okra. Remove tops from the okra just above where cap meets the vegetable. Slice the sausage into 1" pieces.

- Heat 1 tbsp of oil in a nonstick skillet over medium-high heat. Add the sausage and cook, stirring regularly, until browning and just barely pink in the center. Add the peeled, diced jicama and cook about two more minutes. Add the okra, garlic, and red pepper flakes, tossing to coat everything in the cooking fat.

- Continue cooking and stirring for another four to five minutes until the okra and jicama are browned and tender with just a bit of crunch. Salt and pepper to taste.

- Toast the bread and spread with ½ tsp olive oil, salt and pepper (optional). Plate the skillet meal and squeeze on a bit of lemon juice. Serve with a cut, fresh grapefruit on the side.

Coconut-Peach Quinoa

When you're making a meal with quinoa, it's always a good idea to make extra. You can seal uneaten portions in zip-top freezer bags or airtight containers. They'll stay good refrigerated up to a week or frozen up to four weeks. Having cooked grains on hand makes meal time a snap!

You can find coconut butter (also called coconut cream) in most health food stores. You can substitute coconut oil, but it will give your dish a slightly more oily texture.

- ✓ ½ cup cooked quinoa
- ✓ 1 cup diced peaches, fresh or frozen
- ✓ 1/3 cup unsweetened almond milk
- ✓ 1 tbsp coconut butter
- ✓ 2 drops liquid Vanilla Stevia (or regular)
- ✓ ¼ tsp ground nutmeg
- ✓ 2 cups carrot and celery sticks

- Place the quinoa, diced peaches, almond milk, coconut butter, stevia and nutmeg in a small pot or microwave-safe dish.

- Mix the ingredients and cook over low heat on the stovetop, stirring constantly, for about five minutes or until hot. Alternately, cover and microwave on high for about two minutes and stir.

- Serve with a side of carrot and celery sticks.

Savory Sunny-Side-Up Oatmeal

Savory Sunny-Side-Up Oatmeal

Oatmeal doesn't have to be sweet! In this savory oatmeal dish, we replace the cooking water with chicken stock, making breakfast burst with flavor. The vegetables cook right along with the oats, and the egg on top adds some creaminess, texture, and protein. Bon appetite.

- ✓ ½ cup chicken stock
- ✓ 1 cup baby spinach
- ✓ ½ cup sliced button mushrooms
- ✓ ¼ cup old-fashioned or rolled oats
- ✓ ¼ cup diced white onion
- ✓ 1 clove garlic, crushed
- ✓ 2 tsp sesame oil, divided
- ✓ 1 medium whole egg (not Jumbo or Large)
- ✓ Sea salt and cracked black pepper to taste
- ✓ 1 cup Phase 3 fruit

- Heat one teaspoon of sesame oil in a saucepan set over medium heat. Add the mushrooms, onion, and garlic and cook until fragrant (about three minutes), stirring regularly. Add chicken stock and rolled oats to the pot and bring to a boil. Reduce to a high simmer and cook for about five minutes or until oats are tender and stock is absorbed.

- While the oats simmer, heat the other teaspoon of sesame oil in a nonstick skillet over medium heat. Crack the egg into a small dish, then pour it gently onto the heated oil. Cook until the whites are done but the yolk is still soft and runny.

- Pour the savory oats into a bowl and top with the sunny-side-up egg. Salt and pepper to taste. Serve with a side of Phase 3 fruit.

Zucchini & Hazelnut Bread

Zucchini & Hazelnut Bread [serves 3]

PREP TIME: 15 MIN, TOTAL TIME: 75 MIN

This bread tastes like the zucchini bread you remember, but it's full of flavor without the harmful sugars, fat, or wheat flour. This recipe calls for a loaf pan, but a Bundt pan works just as well and makes this sweet bread look like a coffee cake! If you're making it only for yourself, wrap the remaining portions and refrigerate. You'll have breakfast for the next two days of Phase 3.

- ✓ 6 cups shredded zucchini
- ✓ 1 cup tapioca starch
- ✓ 3/4 cup uncooked whole rolled oats
- ✓ ¾ cup Hazelnut meal
- ✓ ½ cup birch xylitol
- ✓ 1 whole egg
- ✓ ¼ cup unsweetened almond milk

- ✓ 2 tbsp coconut oil, divided
- ✓ 1 tsp baking soda
- ✓ 1 tsp cinnamon
- ✓ ½ tsp baking powder
- ✓ ¼ tsp salt
- ✓ 3 cups or 3 pieces of Phase 3 fruit

- Preheat oven to 350°F. Grease a 5 x 9" loaf pan with ½ tbsp. of coconut oil. Set aside.

- In a medium-sized bowl, mix together the tapioca starch, hazelnut meal, oats, baking soda, baking powder, cinnamon, and salt. Set aside. In a larger bowl, mix together the shredded zucchini, xylitol, egg, almond milk, and 1 ½ tbsp. coconut oil (melted) until everything is wet and zucchini has released some of its moisture.

- Slowly add the dry ingredients to the wet, mixing thoroughly. You may add a bit more almond milk or water if the batter is getting too thick. Pour into prepared loaf pan and bake in the preheated oven for 50 – 60 minutes or until a toothpick inserted into the center comes out clean. The loaf will be browned and should spring back when pressed with your finger. Remove to a bakery rack to cool.

- Slice into three sections and serve warm with a side of Phase 3 fruit.

Granola & Bacon – Topped Sweet Potato

PREP TIME: 15 MIN,   BAKE TIME: 1 HOUR

It may seem like an unlikely combination, but the crunchy granola and smoky bacon bits are fine compliments to the humble sweet potato. Put everything together at once and it all comes out at the same time, ready to assemble!

- ✓ 1 medium sweet potato

- ✓ 3 strips turkey bacon

- ✓ ¼ cup uncooked old fashioned oats

- ✓ 1 tbsp coconut oil, melted

- ✓ 1 tsp birch xylitol

- ✓ ½ tsp cinnamon

- ✓ Pinch salt

- ✓ 1 cup Phase 3 Fruit for serving

- Preheat oven to 350°F.

- Scrub the sweet potato and pierce the skin several times with a fork. Wrap in foil and place in the center rack of the preheated oven. Set the timer for one hour.

- In a small bowl, mix together oats, coconut oil, xylitol, cinnamon, and salt. Spread mixture on a small parchment-lined cookie sheet or metal pie pan and place in the oven. Stir every fifteen minutes to crisp evenly.

- When there are fifteen minutes left on the timer, lay the bacon strips on a foil-lined pan and place them in the oven. They should be crisp when the timer runs out. Remove the bacon to a cutting board and set the granola on a trivet to cool.

- Unwrap the potato and place it on the serving plate. Split it down the center and open it up, being careful of the steam. Mash the inside slightly with a fork.

- Chop the bacon and sprinkle the bits on the potato along with the granola. Serve with a side of Phase 3 fruit.

PHASE ③ ... LUNCH TIME!

Tex-Mex Chicken Lettuce Wraps

PREP TIME: 5 MIN, TOTAL TIME: 5 MIN

With some leftover cooked chicken on hand, these delicious wraps come together in minutes! When you're choosing lettuce for wraps, try to find heads that have broad leaves without tears. Red and green leaf lettuces and butter lettuce all work well.

- ✓ 4 oz leftover grilled or roasted chicken, chopped
- ✓ 3/4 cup tomato, seeded and diced
- ✓ 10 black olives, pitted and sliced
- ✓ 1 tbsp diced green chilies
- ✓ 2 green onions, pale and light green parts only, sliced
- ✓ 1 garlic clove, crushed
- ✓ ½ tsp each: cumin, smoked paprika, chili powder
- ✓ 1 lime wedge
- ✓ 3 tbsp shredded vegan cheddar cheese
- ✓ 3 – 4 large lettuce leaves, rinsed and dried
- ✓ 1 cup Phase 3 fruit

- In a medium bowl, mix together diced tomato, olives, green chilies, green onions, garlic and spices.

- Divide the chicken and salsa evenly between the lettuce leaves. Squeeze on the lime juice and sprinkle with vegan shredded cheese.

- Roll into "wraps." Serve with a side of Phase 3 Fruit, such as a cup of mixed blackberries, blueberries, and raspberries.

Vegetarian Lentil & Kale Stew [serves 2]

PREP TIME: 5 MIN, TOTAL TIME: 20 MIN

A new take on an old vegetarian classic, this thick and rich lentil stew adds the superfood kale to create a hearty meal that comes together in minutes. Make it lunch for two, or freeze one portion for a Phase 3 lunch next week!

- ✓ 3/4 cup canned or cooked lentils, rinsed
- ✓ 1 1/2 cups vegetable broth
- ✓ ½ cup diced white onion
- ✓ 2 cloves garlic
- ✓ 1 large carrot, peeled and diced
- ✓ 1 celery stalk, trimmed and diced
- ✓ 2 cups packed washed baby kale
- ✓ 1 tbsp coconut vinegar
- ✓ 2 tbsp olive oil
- ✓ Sea salt to taste
- ✓ 2 cups Phase 3 fruit

- In a medium saucepan, heat oil over medium heat. Add the onion, garlic, carrot and celery. Cook for about three minutes or until the vegetables are fragrant and the onion is translucent.

- Add vegetable broth and simmer about five minutes. Add lentils and cook another three to five minutes until stew begins to thicken and bubble.

- Stir in the kale and cook, stirring, about two minutes until kale is wilted and tender. Stir in vinegar. Salt to taste and serve hot with one cup Phase 3 fruit per serving.

Ginger Lemon Shrimp & Chicory Salad

Ginger Lemon Shrimp & Chicory Salad

Salad shrimp are small, bite-sized shrimp that generally come precooked, packed flash-frozen and ready to eat! Because there's no cooking involved, this light, fresh salad comes together in minutes and gives you a low-fat, low calorie, protein packed meal.

- ✓ 2 cups packed chicory (curly endive) leaves, torn
- ✓ 4 oz frozen salad shrimp (cooked, deveined, tails removed)
- ✓ ¼ cup bean sprouts
- ✓ ¼ cup shredded carrots
- ✓ 1 cup or piece of Phase 3 fruit of your choosing

Dressing:

- ✓ 1 tbsp grapeseed oil
- ✓ 1 garlic clove, minced
- ✓ 1 tsp fresh grated ginger
- ✓ ¼ tsp white pepper
- ✓ Juice of ¼ lemon
- ✓ Pinch of sea salt

- Defrost the shrimp in the refrigerator overnight, or place in a colander and run under cold water until defrosted.

- Remove the leaves from the ribs. Discard ribs and tear the leaves into bite-sized pieces. Lay the torn chicory onto a plate.

- Whisk together all the dressing ingredients in a medium bowl. Add shrimp, carrots and bean sprouts and toss to completely coat. Pour the dressed shrimp and vegetables onto the plated lettuce.

- Serve with one cup Phase 3 fruit.

Hearty Coconut Lobster Bisque [serves 4]

PREP TIME: 15 MIN, TOTAL TIME: 40 MIN

Coconut milk gives this bisque a nice, sweet flavor that works well with the tender lobster. Instead of making a rue to thicken the soup, this steers clear of flours by blending some of the cooked vegetables as a thickener. Be sure to use the canned, full-fat coconut milk and not the refrigerated milk in a carton.

- ✓ 1 ½ cups cooked lobster meat, fresh or frozen (thawed and shredded)
- ✓ 4 cups lobster stock (preferred), fish stock, or chicken stock
- ✓ 2 cups unsweetened canned coconut milk (full fat)
- ✓ 2 cups diced jicama
- ✓ 3/4 cup diced celery
- ✓ ½ cup finely diced white onion
- ✓ 2- 3 carrots, finely diced

- ✓ 1 tbsp tomato paste
- ✓ 1 tbsp coconut oil
- ✓ 1 tsp Simply Organic All Purpose Seasoning
- ✓ ¼ tsp each: cinnamon, crushed red pepper flakes, dry mustard powder
- ✓ Fresh thyme sprigs and lemon wedge for garnish
- ✓ 4 cups Phase 3 fruit

- In a large stock pot, heat the oil over medium heat. Add the onion, jicama, celery, and carrots. Cook, stirring regularly, for about five minutes or until onions are translucent and fragrant. Add the lobster stock and bring to a boil. Reduce heat and simmer about ten to fifteen minutes until jicama and carrots are softened.

- Using a slotted spoon, remove about 1 ½ cups of the cooked vegetables to a high powered blender. Add one cup of the broth and blend until smooth. Pour this puree back into the pot.

- Add the coconut milk, lobster, tomato paste and seasonings and stir until well mixed. Simmer on low another ten minutes or more for flavors to meld.

- Serve hot with fresh thyme, lemon wedges, and one cup Phase 3 fruit.

Quick Garlic Guacamole and Crudités [serves 2]

PREP TIME: 5 MIN, TOTAL TIME: 5 MIN

There's nothing better than the simple flavor of fresh guacamole. Remember to make just enough for you to eat, or share, in one sitting as avocado goes brown very quickly. However, you can prolong the browning process by saving the pit and placing it in the middle of your guacamole before sealing in an airtight container.

- ✓ 1 ripe avocado
- ✓ ½ cup canned organic white beans, drained
- ✓ 1 large garlic clove, finely minced
- ✓ 1 tbsp minced red onion
- ✓ 1 tbsp chopped fresh cilantro
- ✓ Juice of ¼ lime
- ✓ 4 cups cut raw vegetables for dipping, such as carrot and celery sticks and sliced cucumber
- ✓ 2 cups Phase 3 fruit

- Cut the avocado in half around the pit. Scoop out the pit and discard.

- With a small metal spoon, scoop out the avocado flesh into a small bowl. Add the beans, garlic, onion, cilantro, and lime juice and smash with a fork until the avocado and beans are mashed with just a few chunks.

- Serve with cut raw vegetables for dipping and a side of Phase 3 fruit.

Egg-Salad Stuffed Tomatoes

Egg-Salad Stuffed Tomatoes

PREP TIME: 5 MIN, TOTAL TIME: 5 MIN

This egg salad cup is easy to make and easy to pack for a lunch at work. Instead of bread, the salad is stuffed into a hollowed tomato and topped with tender watercress. It's great to keep boiled eggs on hand for a quick protein meal or snack.

- ✓ 1 large ripe tomato
- ✓ 1 whole boiled egg
- ✓ 1 tbsp safflower mayonnaise
- ✓ ½ tsp prepared yellow mustard
- ✓ Sea salt and black pepper to taste
- ✓ Pinch of paprika
- ✓ 1 cup watercress
- ✓ 1 cup Phase 3 fruit

- Cut the tomato in half and scoop out the center. Set aside.

- In a small bowl, mash together the eggs, mayonnaise, mustard, salt and black pepper. Scoop half of the egg mixture into each tomato cup.

- Sprinkle paprika and top with rinsed and dried watercress. Serve with one cup Phase 3 fruit.

Roasted Veggie and Sausage Jumble [serves 2]

PREP TIME: 5 MIN, TOTAL TIME: 1 HOUR

You can make this dish with almost any Phase 3 head or root vegetable, such as jicama, yams, asparagus, carrots, radishes or leeks. Just cut up the veggies, toss them in oil and slip them in the oven to bake. Your sausage cooks right in the same pan, making cleanup a snap.

- ✓ 1 green pepper
- ✓ 1 red pepper
- ✓ 1 cup broccoli florets
- ✓ 1 cup cauliflower florets
- ✓ 1 red onion, cut into wedges
- ✓ 2 fresh or smoked turkey sausages (at least 3 oz. each) , cut into 2" pieces
- ✓ 2 tablespoons olive oil
- ✓ ½ tsp each dried oregano, garlic powder, dried basil, paprika, black pepper
- ✓ 1 tsp sea salt
- ✓ 2 cups Phase 3 fruit

Optional dipping sauce:

- ✓ 3 tbsp safflower mayonnaise whisked with ½ tsp cumin

- Preheat oven to 375°F.

- Trim the peppers, remove seeds and slice into wedges. Peel the onion and slice into wedges.

- Toss everything into a big bowl and turn to coat completely with spices and oil. Spread in an even layer on a rimmed nonstick baking sheet and bake for about an hour, turning several times until the veggies are slightly charred and sausage is cooked through.

- Serve hot with a side of Phase 3 fruit.

PHASE ③ ...
DINNER IS SERVED!

Slow Cooker Bolognese [serves 4]

If you want pasta without the grains, try Yam Noodles. You can find them at most health food or stores in the refrigerated section, at Japanese groceries, or order them online! Or you can serve your pasta over cooked spaghetti squash.

- ✓ 1 lb lean ground beef
- ✓ 1 28 oz can plum tomatoes
- ✓ 6 oz tomato sauce
- ✓ 1 large white onion, diced
- ✓ 2 carrots, peeled and shredded
- ✓ 1 celery stalk, chopped
- ✓ ½ lb button mushrooms, chopped
- ✓ 2 cloves garlic, crushed

- ✓ ½ cup chicken stock
- ✓ 1 tsp olive oil
- ✓ 1 tsp dried basil
- ✓ ½ tsp dried oregano
- ✓ Sea salt to taste
- ✓ 2 cups cooked quinoa or quinoa pasta (optional)

- Sautee the onions and garlic in the olive oil in a saucepan set over medium heat until onion is translucent and garlic is fragrant, (about three minutes). Place into the slow cooker.

- Using the same pan, brown the ground beef and drain excess fat. Add beef and all remaining ingredients (except quinoa or pasta) to the slow cooker and mix thoroughly.

- Place the lid on the slow cooker and cook on high about five hours (low for up to eight hours), or until vegetables are tender.

- Serve alone or atop cooked quinoa or 100% quinoa pasta, yam noodles or spaghetti squash.

Almond Chicken Thighs & Cauliflower Whip

Almond Chicken Thighs & Cauliflower Whip

[serves 4]

PREP: 10 MIN, TOTAL: 45 MIN

Chicken thighs are just as delicious and easy to cook as the breasts, and the serving size is perfect for this dish. Whipped cauliflower has the lovely consistency of tender mashed potatoes, just make sure you cook it until extremely tender or you'll end up with a grainy mash.

For Almond Chicken:

- ✓ 4 chicken thighs
- ✓ 1 egg, beaten
- ✓ ¼ cup almond meal (ground almonds)
- ✓ 1 tsp sea salt

For Whipped Cauliflower:

- ✓ 1 head cauliflower, steam and leaves removed
- ✓ 1 tsp olive oil
- ✓ ½ tsp each: sea salt, garlic powder, cracked black pepper
- ✓ 4 cups steamed green beans, for serving

- Preheat oven to 375°F. Dredge the chicken thighs in the egg, then roll in the almond meal. Place them in an even layer in a glass baking pan. Cover tightly with aluminum foil and bake for about 30 minutes or until juices run clear.

- Meanwhile, cut the cauliflower into chunks and place in a steamer basket set over a pot of water. Bring to a boil. Steam for about 10 – 15 minutes or until cauliflower is so tender it falls apart when stabbed with a fork.

- Place cooked cauliflower into your food processor with 1 tsp olive oil and spices. Puree until smooth. Serve alongside the baked chicken.

- For additional vegetables, add one cup each of steamed green beans. Enjoy!

Black Bean & Sweet Potato Burritos [serves 2]

PREP TIME: 10 MIN,   TOTAL TIME: 10 MIN

Canned refried beans are a quick and easy protein. Mix them with cooked, mashed sweet potato to bulk up the veggie intake and add a surprisingly delicious flavor. If you don't have cooked sweet potato on hand, prick one all over with a fork and microwave for about twelve minutes until it's very soft. The skin will slide right off.

- ✓ 3/4 cup refried black beans (canned, organic vegetarian)
- ✓ 1 cup cooked mashed sweet potato
- ✓ ½ cup prepared fresh salsa
- ✓ ¼ cup prepared guacamole
- ✓ 2 tbsp vegan cheddar cheese (optional)
- ✓ 1 cup shredded Romaine lettuce
- ✓ 1 tsp cumin
- ✓ ½ tsp oregano
- ✓ ½ tsp garlic powder
- ✓ ½ tsp sea salt
- ✓ 2 sprouted grain tortillas

- Mix together the refried beans, mashed sweet potato (no peels), and spices in a small pot set over medium heat. Cook, stirring, about five minutes or until hot.

- Spread half of the bean and sweet potato mixture onto each of the tortillas. Top with guacamole, vegan cheddar cheese, fresh salsa and shredded lettuce.

- Roll and enjoy!

Coconut Shrimp with Cilantro & Lime Slaw
[serves 3]

PREP TIME: 15 MIN, TOTAL: 30 MIN

If you love the coconut shrimp you get as an appetizer at restaurants, you'll love this healthier take on a treasured favorite. If you want to save time on the slaw, you can purchase bagged shredded cabbage that is already "slaw-ready!"

For the shrimp:

- ✓ 1 lb uncooked medium shrimp (deveined, tails removed)
- ✓ ¾ cup unsweetened coconut flakes
- ✓ ¼ cup coconut flour
- ✓ 1 egg, beaten
- ✓ Salt and pepper to taste

For the slaw:

- ✓ 1 small head red or green cabbage
- ✓ 2 green onions, sliced
- ✓ ¼ cup chopped cilantro
- ✓ 1 clove garlic, minced
- ✓ Juice of one lime
- ✓ 1 tsp birch xylitol
- ✓ Sea salt and pepper to taste

- Preheat oven to 375°F. Line a baking sheet with lightly greased parchment paper. Set aside.

- Rinse and dry the shrimp with paper towels. Add salt and pepper to the beaten egg. Place the coconut flour in one bowl and shredded coconut in another. Dredge the shrimp one at a time first in the coconut flour, then the egg, then the shredded coconut and set on a plate to rest for ten minutes.

- Lay shrimp in a single layer on the prepared pan and bake for 10 – 13 minutes until shrimp is pink and coconut is crisped.

- While the shrimp is baking, make the slaw: Remove the stem of the cabbage head and finely shred the leaves with a sharp knife. Place in a large bowl and add the green onion. Whisk together lime juice, garlic, xylitol, and cilantro.

- Toss with the cabbage mixture and serve chilled.

Fennel Stuffed Cornish Game Hens

Fennel Stuffed Cornish Game Hens [serves 2]

PREP TIME: 10 MIN,   TOTAL TIME: 1 HR

Cornish game hens may seem like a delicacy, but they are actually quite simple to prepare. By stuffing them with vegetables, you add moisture and flavor. The olive oil helps crisp up the skin while the meat is kept savory and tender.

- ✓ 2 whole fresh Cornish game hens
- ✓ 2 carrots, finely diced
- ✓ 2 stalks celery, diced
- ✓ 1 small yellow onion, diced
- ✓ ¼ cup diced fennel bulb
- ✓ 1 cup chicken broth
- ✓ 1 tsp Simply Organic Seasoning
- ✓ 1 tsp sea salt
- ✓ 1 tbsp olive oil
- ✓ 2 cups steamed green beans, for serving

- Preheat oven to 425°F. In a small bowl, mix together the vegetables.

- Stuff half of the vegetable mixture into the cavity of each of the game hens.

- Rub the skin of the hens with olive oil, then rub in salt and Simply Organic Seasoning. Place the stuffed hens on a roasting rack in a roasting pan. Pour the chicken broth into the pan and cover.

- Bake in the preheated oven for 30 minutes.

- Remove lid, baste, and continue roasting another thirty minutes until skin is crisp. Serve with a side of steamed green beans.

Baked Chicken, Wild Rice, and Artichokes [serves 4]

PREP TIME: 10 MIN,   TOTAL: 55 MIN

This is a fantastic dish to prepare for a family dinner or when you're expecting company. The creamy sauce tastes great with the wild rice and vegetables. The best part is that \everything goes together in one casserole dish, making cleanup easy.

- ✓ 4 small chicken breasts

- ✓ 1 cup uncooked wild rice

- ✓ 3 cups artichoke hearts, frozen (thawed)

- ✓ 1 cup diced red pepper

- ✓ 1 cup frozen chopped spinach, thawed

- ✓ 3 cups chicken broth

- ✓ 3 tbsp tapioca starch

- ✓ 2 tbsp olive oil, divided

- ✓ 2 tsp sea salt

- ✓ ½ tsp each: dried oregano, basil, garlic powder, dried mustard powder, cracked black pepper, onion powder, crushed red pepper flakes (optional)

- ✓ 1 tsp paprika

- Preheat oven to 375°F. In the bottom of a large casserole dish greased with 1 tbsp olive oil, mix together wild rice and tapioca starch.

- Rub the chicken breasts with the remaining tablespoon of olive oil.

- Mix in remaining ingredients, except chicken breasts and paprika, until everything is well-coated. Nestle the chicken breasts on top of the mixture and sprinkle with paprika and a little sea salt.

- Cover and bake 45 – 55 minutes until rice is tender, sauce has thickened, and chicken breasts are tender and juices run clear.

Crab Cake Over Wilted Spinach & Fennel

PREP TIME: 5 MIN, TOTAL TIME: 10 MIN

Crab for breakfast? Absolutely. You won't be crabby with this little seafood cake on top of a toasted English muffin. With just a handful of ingredients, your breakfast table turns gourmet, even if it's just a table for one.

- ✓ 4 oz lump crab meat
- ✓ 1 egg
- ✓ ½ tbsp. olive oil
- ✓ 1 green onion, diced
- ✓ ½ tsp prepared horseradish
- ✓ Pinch of sea salt and pepper

- ✓ 2 cups washed baby spinach
- ✓ 1 small fennel bulb
- ✓ 1 lemon wedge, plus one for serving (optional)
- ✓ ½ sprouted grain English muffin (optional grain)

- In a small bowl, smash together the crab meat, diced green onion, horseradish, and pinch of salt and pepper. Add the egg and mix to form a sticky dough.

- Trim the fennel and thinly slice the onion-like bulb. Set aside.

- Coat a small nonstick pan in the olive oil and set over medium heat.

- Form the crab mixture into a patty and lay onto the hot oil. Fry until browned on the underside, about two minutes. Flip and fry the other side to golden brown. Remove to a paper towel. Keep the pan over the heat.

- Add the fennel to the pan and sauté, stirring regularly, about one minute. Add spinach to the pan with a squeeze of lemon juice. Cook for one to two minutes, turning a few times, until the spinach is just wilted.

- Spoon the spinach and fennel onto the serving plate (or atop a toasted English muffin) and top with the crab cake. Serve with an additional lemon wedge (optional).

PHASE ③ ...
TIME FOR SNACKS!

Sunny Celery Sticks

This dip is a different take on the classic peanut butter and celery snack you may have enjoyed as a kid. You can make up a larger batch and keep cut veggies in the fridge for a quick snack any time during Phase 3.

- ✓ 3 – 4 celery stalks
- ✓ 3 tbsp raw sunflower seed butter
- ✓ 2 – 3 drop liquid stevia (optional)
- ✓ Dash cinnamon

- Clean the celery and cut it lengthwise down the center, and then into 3" sticks.

- In a small bowl, stir together the sunflower seed butter, stevia, and cinnamon.

- Serve the celery alongside the sunflower dip.

Liver and Onion Stuffed Mushrooms

Liver and Onion Stuffed Mushrooms

PREP TIME: 10 MIN, TOTAL TIME: 30 MIN

This dish takes a little bit of extra time, but it's a great recipe to triple and serve as an appetizer when you have guests. The liver is tender and rich, while the mushrooms make a perfect two-bite container to hold everything together.

- ✓ 4 oz calf's liver
- ✓ 1 small yellow onion, finely diced
- ✓ 5 large button mushroom caps
- ✓ 1 tbsp olive oil
- ✓ 1 clove garlic, minced
- ✓ Pinch of sea salt and black pepper
- ✓ Preheat the oven to 350°F.

- Clean and dry the mushrooms and remove stems, placing the caps top-down on a rimmed baking pan. Mince the stems and set aside.

- In a large nonstick skillet, bring the olive oil to medium-high heat. Add the onion and garlic. Sautee about five minutes, stirring regularly, until onions are translucent and garlic is fragrant.

- Move the onion to one side of the pan and add the diced liver and minced mushroom to the open space. Let this fry for about three minutes, then mix everything together. Reduce heat, cover and simmer about ten minutes until liver is done brown and tender. Salt and pepper to taste.

- Scoop heaping tablespoons of the mixture evenly into the mushroom caps. Use more mushrooms if you have excess mixture. Bake in the preheated oven for about twenty minutes, until mushrooms are wilted and juice is pooling in the pan underneath. Serve hot.

Quick Pesto Hummus and Veggies

Quick Pesto Hummus and Veggies [serves 4]

This recipe puts an Italian twist on a Mediterranean favorite! Just remember, fresh basil makes a big difference. Don't skimp here and use dried, it won't taste the same. If you're really in a hurry, don't divide the pine nuts and oil Just throw everything right in the food processor.

- ✓ 1 cup drained and rinsed canned garbanzo beans
- ✓ 8 fresh basil leaves
- ✓ 1 large clove garlic, crushed
- ✓ 2 tbsp pine nuts, divided
- ✓ 3 tsp olive oil, divided
- ✓ 2 tbsp lemon juice
- ✓ ¼ tsp sea salt
- ✓ Any Phase 3 veggies, washed and sliced

- Place the garbanzo beans, basil leaves, garlic, 1 ½ tablespoons pine nuts, and 2 teaspoons olive oil, lemon juice and salt in the food processor and process until smooth.

- Scoop into a bowl and drizzle with remaining olive oil and sprinkle with remaining pine nuts.

- Serve with any raw Phase 3 veggies.

Lemony Arugula Salad with Cashews

Even though this salad has just a few ingredients, it's packed with flavor. It's light, fresh, and creamy with just the right amount of crunch from the chopped nuts.

- ✓ 2 cups baby arugula, washed and patted dry
- ✓ 2 tbsp cashew butter
- ✓ 1 tbsp lemon juice
- ✓ 2 drops liquid stevia (or to taste)
- ✓ Pinch sea salt
- ✓ 6 cashews, coarsely chopped

- In a small bowl, whisk together the cashew butter, lemon juice, stevia, and sea salt until smooth. Add a bit of water if the consistency is too thick.

- Toss the dressing with the arugula and top with the chopped cashews.

Oven-Baked Jicama Fries

PREP TIME: 5 MIN, TOTAL TIME: 50 MIN

If you love French fries, you are in for a real treat. These jicama fries are crisp on the outside and tender in the middle with just the right amount of salt. You can change up this simple recipe by using coconut oil and adding a bit of cayenne pepper for a sweet & spicy variety.

- ✓ 1 medium jicama
- ✓ 3 tbsp olive oil
- ✓ 1 tsp sea salt

- Preheat the oven to 425°F. Peel the rough skin off the jicama and discard. Cut the jicama into even ¼" wide "fries." Pat dry with paper towels to remove excess water.

- Toss the jicama, olive oil, and sea salt in a large bowl to completely coat. Spread in an even layer, with space between each fry, on a large rimmed nonstick cookie sheet. If you run out of room, use a second sheet.

- Bake 45 minutes until browned and crisp on the outside.

BONUS:
Dessert Anyone?
SWEET ENDINGS!

SWEET ENDINGS

Desserts are *not* off limits on the Fast Metabolism diet! The following dessert ideas fit into their respective phases, and can be used as one of your two snacks or added after a meal. However, if you're adding dessert, you'll need to add a day of exercise to that phase.

Phase 1 Dessert:

Speedy Pineapple Sorbet

PREP TIME: 5 MIN, TOTAL TIME: 5 MIN

Sorbets are simple and come out beautifully if you have a high-powered kitchen blender, such as a Vitamix. You can also try using your food processor, but you may end up with a few lumps. That's okay, sorbet is delicious any way you have it!

- ✓ 1 cup frozen pineapple chunks
- ✓ 1 tbsp birch xylitol
- ✓ 2 tbsp water

- Place all ingredients into your high speed blender and process on high, using your plunger wand to push down the pineapple, until smooth, adding more water if the frozen fruit won't budge. About three minutes.

- Enjoy!

Vanilla-Lime Meringues

Phase 2 Dessert:

Vanilla-Lime Meringues [serves 2]

PREP TIME: 5 MIN,   TOTAL TIME: 4 HOURS

These meringues are so delicious, you won't believe that they're good for you! With just a few minutes of prep, and a little patience, you can have a decadent dessert that tastes like key lime pie!

- ✓ ¾ cup liquid egg white
- ✓ Zest from two limes
- ✓ 1 dropper full of liquid vanilla stevia

- In a standing kitchen mixer, beat the egg whites until stiff peaks form. This part is crucial. If your egg whites are too soft, they won't harden.

- Gently fold in the stevia and lime zest.

- Scoop meringue batter onto a parchment lined tray by the ¼ cup.

- Set aside in a warm, dry place (such as your oven) for about four hours or overnight until the meringues harden.

Phase 3 Dessert:

Sweet Potato Custard Pie

PREP TIME: 5 MIN,   TOTAL TIME: 10 MIN

This quick microwave pie is reminiscent of Thanksgiving with its pumpkin pie spices and creamy sweet filling. If you don't have pecans on hand for the crust, almond meal works just as well.

- ✓ ¾ cup cooked, mashed sweet potato

- ✓ 1 egg, beaten

- ✓ 3 tbsp cup ground pecans (pecan meal)

- ✓ 1 tsp coconut oil

- ✓ ½ packet stevia

- ✓ 1 tablespoon birch xylitol

- ✓ ½ tsp baking powder (gluten and corn free)

- ✓ ½ tsp each: ground cinnamon, nutmeg, vanilla extract

- Mix together the ground pecans, coconut oil, and stevia and press into the bottom of a 4" microwave-safe ramekin.

- In a bowl with a hand mixer, beat together the sweet potato, egg, birch xylitol, baking powder, and spices. Pour over the crust and microwave for about three minutes or until the center is soft-set.

- If you don't want to use a microwave, bake in a preheated 350°F oven for about thirty minutes or until the center is soft-set.

If you found this book helpful, please consider leaving a review at Amazon. I read every one, even if it's just a line or two. ☺ It makes all the difference and is very much appreciated. Thank you!

I truly hope these recipes will help you on your weight loss journey. Good luck and get cooking!

Made in the USA
San Bernardino, CA
05 January 2016